The Secret Joy of Hygge

The Secret Joy of Hygge

A Practical Guide to Cultivating Happiness in the Everyday

ALEXANDRA AMAROTICO

Illustrations by Irena Freitas

ALTHEA
PRESS

Interior and Cover Designer: Will Mack
Photo Art Director: Sue Bischofberger
Editor: Pippa White
Production Editor: Erum Khan
Illustrations © Irena Freitas, 2018
ISBN: Print 978-1-64152-323-3 | eBook 978-1-64152-324-0

To my mother, the most loving, hyggelig person I know.

Contents

Introduction viii

Chapter One
Defining Hygge 1

Chapter Two
Self 21

Chapter Three
Home 51

Chapter Four
Family & Community 81

Chapter Five
Work & Career 109

Resources 139   Index 146

Introduction

I was just 16 when I first stepped foot in Denmark. I was about to begin a yearlong student exchange— though I knew very little about the small Scandinavian country and its culture, and I didn't speak a word of Danish.

As soon as I arrived in Aarhus, Denmark's second largest city, I was struck by its romantic European charms that were so different from the green mountains of Oregon I'd known my whole life. I quickly fell for its rich history, quaint cobblestone streets, tiled rooftops, and sprawling landscapes. Once I'd gotten accustomed to my new physical surroundings, though, I started to feel comfortable and concluded that my life in Denmark *actually* didn't look so different from my life growing up in Oregon after all. Every morning, people headed off to work or school, and in the evenings, children rode bicycles down the street and families gathered around the dinner table. For a while, I took all of this at face value. As time went on, however, and I immersed myself deeper in Danish life, I discovered that there *was* something below the surface that made this new place incredibly special: *hygge*.

Whether it was during music classes in my high school, long drawn-out meals with friends that involved a lot of laughter, or Danish language lessons with my host mother after dinner, I began to notice that the Danes around me had a special ability to find so much joy in the little things. Rarely did these people seem anxious to be somewhere else or worry about the past or the future. Whatever they were doing, they were fully engaged, present, and all in.

I witnessed my host mother reading a captivating book outside on a cold day, staying warm with soft blankets and hot tea. I'd see my new friends traveling quickly and easily by bicycle, appreciating the feeling of the wind in their hair and carrying on a conversation as easily as though they were side by side in a car. Members of the local Rotary Club invited me over to their home for no reason other than to share coffee, cake, and laughter. People would light candles on regular weekday evenings to brighten the mood, instead of saving those candles for "special occasions." Despite the cold weather, there was a constant feeling of warmth, cheer, and gratitude. It was hard to put into words what I was witnessing, but there seemed to be a continuous celebration of the small things. I saw that the Danes weren't waiting for holidays, a big job promotion, or someone's wedding in order to mark time or celebrate what they had. Instead, they continuously celebrated the here and now. They paid attention to the details of their lives, and as a result they felt joy regularly and consistently.

Needless to say, I wanted to know more! I dove headfirst into learning everything I could about hygge. The more I incorporated hygge into my daily routine, the more joyful my life became. I saw it working. It didn't take long for me to fall head over heels for the concept and how life-changing it can be. During my time in Denmark, I learned and practiced this positive, fulfilling way of life to the best of my ability. But perhaps the most amazing part of my journey was returning home to the United States and realizing that you don't need to live in Denmark or be Danish by birth to infuse hygge into

your life! All you need is an open mind and someone to guide you—okay, and maybe a few candles.
In this book, I will be that guide for you—sharing
all that I've learned so you can cultivate joy in your
own life.

The Secret Joy of Hygge will provide you with
everything you need to know about hygge in order
to amplify the joy in your life—day by day—no
matter where you live. Each chapter will cover how
hygge applies to a different area of your life—
whether it's your internal world, your wardrobe, how
you decorate your home, the experiences you have

with your family and community, or the application of a new mind-set to your work and career. Each chapter opens with a discussion about how the values of hygge relate to that particular aspect of your life. Then, you'll learn several ways in which you can easily apply hygge to that area through small changes that will increase your overall happiness and feelings of satisfaction.

While the pronunciation of *hygge* can seem daunting (pronounced hoo-gah, by the way), the feeling it represents is quite the opposite. In its simplest form, hygge gives a name and recognition to the small joys in life, making even the most mundane moments feel warmer and more special.

So pour yourself a cup of hot tea and get comfortable. Welcome to the world of hygge happiness!

Chapter One

Defining Hygge

What Is Hygge Really?

Dating back to the 18th century, the Danish word *hygge* (again, pronounced hoo-gah) cannot be directly translated into English. It compares most closely to our definition of the word *cozy*: giving a feeling of comfort, warmth, and relaxation (according to the *Oxford English Dictionary*). With this understanding, it's no surprise that many of us—Danes included—imagine specific things related to coziness when describing the concept of hygge: flickering candles, hot beverages, pastries, comfortable clothing, thick blankets, and soft socks, to name a few.

These items represent coziness well and do signal a certain traditional Danish style of hygge, though at its core, hygge is much more about a feeling than it is about specific material objects. You can easily incorporate elements of Danish traditions and customs into your daily life, or you can manifest hygge in your own way.

Think of hygge, in its plainest form, as an all-encompassing way to describe the simple things in your life that bring you comfort, warmth, and joy. A picnic at the park in the midst of summer:

hygge. Sipping hot cocoa under a blanket while a snowstorm howls outside: hygge. Gathering around a coffee table to play board games; sending a handwritten card to a loved one for their birthday; or hosting a dinner with friends where everyone catches up on old memories, laughing and smiling ear to ear: all definitely hygge.

The best way to invoke a hygge mood is to simply take notice of the small details that bring you joy and repeat them. At first, hygge might sound self-indulgent. Let me assure you that it's more about setting an intention for your actions

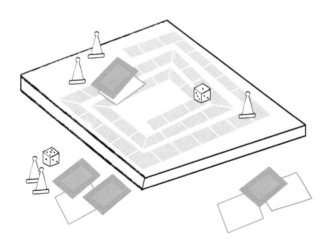

and your mind-set, rather than thoughtlessly indulging in things or overindulging. The difference between self-indulgence and hygge is the difference between mindlessly eating a piece of cake out of boredom, barely tasting it while you watch TV, and eating a piece of cake slowly, savoring each bite, paying attention to how each unique flavor blends into something rich, and thinking about how lucky you are to be able to enjoy such a delicious treat. When we take the time to recognize the things that delight us and provide us with a sense of wonder, instead of just *consuming*, we find ourselves leading happier and more fulfilling lives.

Hygge's Hip

In early 2016, international interest in hygge began to climb. It made the *Oxford English Dictionary*'s shortlist for the word of the year, and the concept was discussed everywhere from *The New Yorker* and *The Washington Post* to NPR and the BBC. Etsy, a website for independent artists, featured a trend report on "hygge products," promoting everything from artisanal coffee to textiles for the home.

And even now, a few years later, an Amazon search for "hygge" will return more than 1,000 results. Clearly, hygge caught our attention and is here to stay.

So why the sudden interest now from Americans? After all, the concept of hygge has been alive and well in Danish culture for centuries. The best answer I can find has to do with the recent evolution of American culture. We've been in the Internet era for just over 25 years—a world where technology dominates our communication, and where we are constantly inundated with information. True, this has affected countries around the world, but it does seem to have had a specific effect on Americans in particular. In 2017, the average American spent nearly three hours on their cell phone each day, and in the same year, American households consumed an average of nearly eight hours of television daily, according to expert measurement and analytics company Comscore. And, unfortunately, these trends only seem to getting more extreme.

According to a 2018 Nielsen Company report in *PC Magazine*, adults in the United States now spend nearly 11 hours per day consuming media

(on our phones, tablets, computers, TVs, etc.). Considering that we need a certain number of hours to sleep out of every 24, that amount of time is staggering—screens truly dominate the average American's life. In the same study, Nielsen found that those who partake in social media spend nearly an hour a day on Instagram and an hour on Facebook. Perhaps unsurprisingly, this constant attachment to devices has been linked to depression and feelings of isolation—not to mention increased health risks to our physical bodies (even cancer, due to the electromagnetic frequency radiation that phone screens emit).

Suffice to say that in this era of over-connection, Americans are discovering that hygge is the perfect antidote for those feelings of detachment from the real world around us. Hygge is not just a lifestyle trend, but also a unique perspective and a way to curate your life around moments of joy. It doesn't require extensive investment, effort, time, or money, but it can help you infuse your life with positivity and feel-good energy all the same.

Key Hygge Terms

To better understand the term *hygge* and how it's used in conversation, you may want to familiarize yourself with these key hygge terms and phrases.

hygger *(pronounced hoo-ger)*: the present-tense verb form of hygge, to experience hygge in the present. *"We hygger right now."*

hyggelig *(pronounced hoo-gah-lee)*/ **hyggeligt** *(pronounced hoo-gah-leet)*: the adverb and adjective form of hygge, used to describe something as encompassing the essence of hygge. "What a hyggelig home you have," or "That party was very hyggeligt!"

hyg dig/kan du hygge dig *(pronounced hoog die/can doo hoo-gah die)*: a friendly farewell or sign-off, similar to *"Have a hygge time!" or "Enjoy yourself!" "Thank you for tonight! Kan du hygge dig!"*

hjemmehygge *(pronounced yem-uh-hoo-gah)*: directly translates to "home hygge" or "hygge at home." *"There are many ways you can increase the hjem-mehygge in your apartment."*

hyggetøj *(pronounced hoo-gah-toy)*: directly translates to "hygge clothing." (It's also worth mentioning a related term: *hygge bukser*, which literally means "hygge pants.") *"I can't wait to go home and put on hyggetøj."*

hyggestund *(pronounced hoo-gah-stund)*: an older term to describe a hyggelig experience. *"What are you guys doing tonight?" "Having a hyggestund."*

hyggespreder *(pronounced hoo-gah-spreler)*: someone or something that contributes to creating a nice, pleasant hygge atmosphere. Candles are a hyg-gespreder, for example, as is a friend who always hosts lovely, cozy gatherings at their home.

"Sara hosts the most wonderful dinner parties—she's definitely a hyggespreder."

hyggestemning *(pronounced hoo-gah-stem-ning)*: directly translates to "hygge mood," denoting a positive mood or having peace of mind. *"Everything about tonight was wonderful—what a hygge-stemning."*

råhygge/rigtig hyggelig *(pronounced row-hoo-gah/wreck-tee hoo-gah-lee)*: directly translates to "raw hygge," or *really* hygge. This is a newer term used to describe a decidedly wonderful, cozy atmosphere. For example, when a terrible snowstorm rages outside but you're inside with a crackling fire and hot cocoa, this is råhygge—hygge at its most extreme. *"This is a rigtig hyggelig party."*

uhyggelig *(pronounced oo-hoo-gah-lee)*: the antonym of hygge, used to describe something that is otherwise uncomfortable or even scary. *"That was such an uhyggelig film."*

lykke *(pronounced loo-kah)*: the Danish word for happiness. For Danes, hygge is an important part of living a lykke life. *"What a lykke day this is!"*

SIMILAR CONCEPTS
AROUND THE WORLD

Just as the English language doesn't have an exact translation for the word hygge, there are a number of other terms from around the world that evoke similar, related sentiments—and are similarly untranslatable.

Fjaka (pronounced f-yaka) is a Croatian word that roughly means relaxing in mind and body and delighting in the feeling of doing nothing.

In Dutch, *gezellig* (pronounced heh-sell-ick) describes the warm feeling you get when spending time with people you care about in a cozy atmosphere.

Fika (pronounced fee-ka), a Swedish term, refers to taking a break during the day for coffee and conversation with a friend or colleague.

Lagom (pronounced lar-gum) is another Swedish word that has recently received attention across the globe. Essentially, it translates to "enough, sufficient, adequate, just right." Instead of too much or too little of something—be it how much time you spend working or how much you eat—practicing lagom means finding a balance and having just enough of what you need to live happily. The idea is that one can more easily achieve happiness and contentment by keeping everything in moderation. The concept of lagom can also be applied to being mindful about personal consumption and taking care of the environment. For example, the Swedish furniture retailer IKEA introduced the Live LAGOM project to help their customers live a "more sustainable, healthy, and cost-conscious life at home."

In Greek, the word *philoxeníā* (pronounced fee-lo-zee-nia) means to welcome strangers into your home with respect and love.

Meanwhile, in Scotland, the Gaelic word *còsagach* (pronounced coze-sag-och) describes the feeling of being sheltered, snug, and cozy. Like hygge, còsagach truly shines in winter, when Scotland's harsh weather makes cuddling up by a fireplace all the more inviting. Spending time in nature and going out to local pubs or restaurants with friends are also key components of a còsagach experience.

What Makes Us Happy?

Experts around the world have extensively researched what makes people happy—and the findings might surprise you.

For example, while external factors do have an impact on our happiness, researchers at the University of Minnesota found that nearly half our happiness is genetically inherited and therefore predetermined from birth. This important information makes it all the more critical that we nurture the happiness that is within our control. That remaining half of our happiness is determined by the choices we make. The way we handle challenging events, who and what we choose to surround ourselves with, and how much we adhere to our own value system—these are the things that determine our expectations and ultimately our overall level of happiness.

The Harvard Study of Adult Development, which tracked the health and aging of participants for over 80 years, found two significant factors that lead to increased happiness. As discussed in *The Harvard Gazette* article covering the study, the first is a focus on close relationships and community, and the second is spending more time doing things that bring us joy. Perhaps unsurprisingly, both of these factors—togetherness and doing things we love—are key aspects of living a hygge life.

But what about our work? In the United States, we tend to place significant value on earned success, with our 9-to-5 work culture taking a place at the forefront of our lives. Many Americans find satisfaction from a hard day's work, as well as an increased level of happiness when they feel that their work provides value for others. Studies actually show that satisfaction at work often brings us more joy than money does. For example, the General Social Survey, which gathers data on several aspects of American life, found that nearly three in four Americans wouldn't quit working even if they were handed enough money to live in luxury for the rest of their lives.

Though they might not admit it at first, many people think more money will bring more happiness. Studies have actually found that this is true—but only to a certain extent. For example, a study at Princeton University reported by *Time* found that Americans are happiest when they earn a salary of around $75,000. Regardless of geographic location (within the United States), the study found that a single person earning $75,000 (or a two-parent family earning $150,000) almost always has enough income that they don't view money as a make-or-break stressful issue— even in cities where the cost of living is very high, like San Francisco and New York*. The study found that people who make this much money generally have enough cash to go out to dinner with friends on occasion, travel, pay their rent or mortgage, and cover other essential costs of living. (Note that for an American family of four, the poverty level is $22,050.)

Now here's the interesting part. The same study found that making much more than $75,000 does not increase happiness—in fact, it could do just the opposite. Anyone making $15,000 to $20,000 more experiences similar happiness effects, but once Americans pass a $95,000 salary, their happiness often actually decreases. The reasons are not

---

* I know, I know—many people living in cities with high costs of living may staunchly take issue with this statement. I am merely reporting what the study found!

precisely known. It could be due to unhealthy social comparisons that can come with increased wealth—trying to keep up with the Joneses, so to speak—or the realization that material possessions don't bring us the joy we expect them to.

Similarly, while we may expect to find long-term happiness after a major positive life event—such as receiving a large raise, moving to a different state, or getting married—studies show this just isn't the case. After an initial spike of joy when something wonderful happens, we quickly adjust to our new normal—a higher income, increased power, being married—and our mood levels off. This indicates that the process of working toward a big reward can often bring us more happiness than actually receiving the reward. The famous Danish philosopher Søren Kierkegaard put it best when he said, "forventningens glæde er den største," which translates to "the joy of expectation is the greatest."

The findings from the Princeton University study illuminate why a hygge mind-set can help us lead happier lives. By slowing down, finding the small joys in each day, and appreciating those little moments as they happen, we are experiencing

anticipation. This enables us to maintain happiness in a more even-keeled way.

As humans, our natural inclination is to avoid change. But if we understand that many factors affect our daily and overall happiness, then we have the opportunity to make small changes that make our lives more meaningful. Even little adjustments to how we approach self-care or putting together our homes, how we handle relationships, and how we regard our careers can increase our feelings of satisfaction. Choosing to enjoy the life we *actually* have—rather than focusing on an idealized version, full of unrealized desires—is the key to living a happy life.

Living a Hygge Life

More than likely, you already incorporate some aspects of hygge into your life without even realizing it. For instance, when you meet a friend for coffee, you may be indulging a hygge feeling. When you take time to write a thank-you note, you're expressing hygge. When you buy flowers on the way home for no particular reason, you're (literally!) taking time out of your busy schedule to stop and smell the roses. This is the essence of hygge—to enjoy your life as it happens and not take for granted the small moments.

Ultimately, no one thing—or even many things—will bring you pure happiness. Your mind-set is the only thing that can turn a regular moment into a moment of joy. A hygge life involves being present and delighting in your world. When you're spending time with friends and laughing so hard that you cry. When you take a walk outside in the middle of a workday and breathe in the fresh air. When you play fetch with your dog and see the pure euphoria in his eyes each time he catches the ball. Strung together, these moments make a more hygge life.

Chapter Two

Self

You, Yourself, and Hygge

While hygge can be applied to every aspect of your life, it's important to understand that living a hygge life starts inside yourself. When you can recognize the hygge moments in each day—and appreciate them in the moment while they are happening—you'll begin to have a more hygge mind-set. Having a good sense of self, knowing what matters most to you, and feeling comfortable in your own skin are key steps to being a hyggelig person.

If all of your basic needs are met—you have food and shelter, and can provide for yourself—how can you shift your mind-set out of survival mode and into focusing on how to take the best care of yourself mentally, emotionally, and physically? In this chapter, we'll explore how things like self-care, grooming, exercise, and meditation play into a hygge life.

To discover your most hygge self, it's important to tune in to your feelings and reactions so you can learn what brings you joy—and what doesn't. You may surprise yourself. While we know that health and wellness are important to living a balanced life, some activities may feel like chores some days—for example, eating well or going to the gym. But there are many ways you can make these aspects of your life more hygge and less routine. Approaching them with a hygge state of mind can help you appreciate and even look forward to these activities, instead of having them be just one more thing you need to get done in a day.

By finding happiness and gratitude within yourself first, you'll be able to apply a hygge mind-set to the rest of your life, including your relationships with others and your work environment. Only by taking care of yourself and accessing your innermost hygge will you be ready to share that hygge feeling with others. It's like television personality RuPaul says: "If you can't love yourself, how in the hell you gonna love somebody else?"

The Art of Self-Care

As stress levels in the United States have climbed in recent years, the concept of self-care has also risen to newfound popularity. According to the Anxiety and Depression Association of America, roughly 40 million Americans have an anxiety disorder.

Likewise, an American Psychiatric Association poll found that an additional 40 percent reported increased levels of stress in 2018. It's no surprise, then, that we are turning to self-care to prioritize our bodies and minds, de-stress, and find ways to increase our happiness and productivity.

For anyone unfamiliar with the term, *self-care* describes taking actions to improve one's general health and well-being. It can refer to any number of activities, products, and experiences. Many use the term to describe things that bring them a feeling of peace or joy—whether that's taking a morning yoga class or using a new skin-care product.

Like hygge, the concept of self-care is not a new one. Their recent parallel ride to fame makes sense—after all, a Sunday evening at home with a face mask and Netflix could be described as both self-care and hygge. While the terms are not interchangeable, most self-care activities could be described as hyggelige (the plural form of hyggelig), and practicing self-care is an important part of a hygge life.

Think of things you do and/or buy solely because they make your mind and body feel happier and healthier. These can be considered forms of self-care, and small adjustments can make them all the more hyggelige. For example:

- Spend a Sunday evening at home with no agenda other than to relax. Watch your favorite feel-good movie or read a new book. Bonus points if you light a few candles, put on a face mask, or pour yourself a cup of tea or a glass of wine.

- Instead of rushing to grab coffee on your way to work, give yourself an extra 10 minutes to actually sit at your favorite café and enjoy your drink at a table. While you do, you can write a list of your goals for the day or listen to an inspiring podcast. Building just this small amount of time into your morning routine will affect your day profoundly by starting it on a positive and relaxed note instead of a chaotic one.

- Set aside time for a "date" with yourself to do things that bring you joy. Treat yourself to an afternoon at a spa, walk through your favorite museum and have a long lunch, or go on a hike or day trip to somewhere you love.

Baths, Saunas, and Massages

One of the host families I lived with during my first year in Denmark had a house near a beautiful lake. Every morning, my host mother would go swimming at sunrise—even though it was January and far below freezing.

While outdoor winter bathing may not sound hyggelig at first, the benefits are widely recognized throughout Scandinavia and are an important part of Scandinavians' health and wellness routines. Studies have indicated that those who regularly swim in cold water tend to be more resistant to cold, handle stress better, and have lower blood pressure overall. Furthermore, your endorphins sky-rocket after winter bathing, which increases your happiness and makes your return to a warm, hygge place all the more wonderful.

In Scandinavian culture, hot springs and baths are also an important part of people's overall wellness and relaxation. Traditional baths and saunas give you the opportunity to alternate between hot, cold, and moderate temperatures. The experience is refreshing and rejuvenating and is said to help decrease stress overall.

Incorporating baths and saunas into your schedule is a great way to make your self-care routine all the more hygge. Of course, we don't all have the luxury of living by a beautiful lake or being able to build a sauna into our homes, but many gyms now offer steam rooms, pools, or saunas, so consider joining one that has these and adding them to your regular workouts. If your gym doesn't have

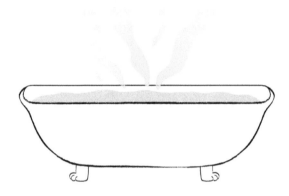

these services, look for bathhouses or spas in your area and see if they sell packages or memberships. Even visiting just once a month can help you relax, unwind, and feel refreshed.

When you go, be sure to alternate temperatures—from warm (in a hot tub or sauna) to cold. Even 2 to 10 seconds in the cold can help rid your body of toxins, close your pores, and boost your energy. Then, go back to moderate heat to let your body relax. Repeat going through these temperatures a few times, and not only will you have a hyggelig experience, but you might just leave feeling a new kind of mental clarity.

Massages are also a wonderful way to treat yourself, relax, and de-stress. With the rise of self-care, massages have become more mainstream and affordable, so finding ways to incorporate them into your life on a regular basis is easier than ever before. Massages might sound self-indulgent, but they can truly make a difference in your mental and physical health. Try it next time you've had a tough week or are feeling particularly tense.

If you want to make your spa experience even more hygge, invite a friend to join you. This may sound odd to Americans, but Danes consider socializing while relaxing to be completely normal. Instead of going out for brunch or happy hour, spend an afternoon at a bathhouse together or sign up for massages at the same time. It's sure to be both hyggelig and fun for both of you.

Creative Expression

In *Big Magic*, author Elizabeth Gilbert urges her readers to listen to the voice inside them that longs to be creative and make wonderful things. "The universe buries strange jewels deep within us all, and then stands back to see if we can find them," she says.

Finding these jewels in yourself, tapping into your creative side, and pursuing what you're most passionate about are essential elements of a hygge life. Whether you love painting, journaling, sewing, gardening, knitting, singing, writing poetry, or any other creative endeavor, making time to pursue that thing can bring you incredible happiness and even a sense of community.

To start pursuing your creative passion, you need to do just that: start. Whether you want to learn something you've never tried before or you're well-versed in something and want to embark on a

new creative project, beginning can seem daunting. To make this process easier, try to let go of your expectations and focus on the feeling of joy you'll have when you're in the process of creating something. It doesn't matter if you knit a single sock or a complicated sweater, or paint on a postcard or a large, expansive canvas. The *experience* of creating, not the result, is the most hygge thing, and will bring you the most joy. (Remember the study I mentioned earlier that found that people are happier when they're in the process of achieving a goal, rather than when they have achieved it?)

You may already have a creative passion in mind. If so, be sure to make time for it in your schedule. Maybe you'll need to wake up 30 minutes earlier in the morning to write before you begin your day. Or perhaps you can spend a Sunday afternoon painting in the sunlight instead of doing something social. If you have a family and need help making time for creative expression in your busy life, try treating it the way you treat other commitments. Add it to your calendar or set a reminder, and don't push it aside for something else. Make an appointment with yourself that you can't wait to keep.

If you're not sure which creative passion to follow, there are many ways to discover new endeavors and opportunities. Today, experts teach online classes about every discipline you can think of—flower arranging, embroidery, cooking, drawing, and much, much more. If you want to discover a new passion in person, look for classes locally— perhaps in pottery, photography, or improv acting.

Finding something that excites or intrigues you and making time to create will help you live a more balanced, joyful, and hygge life. And you never know—you may even discover your true calling while you're at it.

Meditation and Mindfulness

As our level of anxiety has increased in the United States, it's no wonder that interest in and the practice of meditation has gone up as well. Meditation involves focusing your mind in order to clear your head, relax, or find spiritual clarity. Regular meditation has been linked to boosting health, happiness, self-control, productivity, and much more.

Practiced in several cultures for thousands of years, meditation has recently seen a surge in popularity. According to a National Health Interview Survey, more than 18 million Americans are reported to practice meditation, and that number continues to grow.

Meditation helps you clear your thoughts and live in the present, so it's easy to see how the practice can be a hyggelig experience. If you are fully in the moment—not looking backward at stressors or forward to expectations—you can better recognize and appreciate the simple, hygge moments of life as they happen.

If you've never tried meditation, you can start simply by making yourself comfortable in a quiet space. Close your eyes and practice quieting and slowing your thoughts and mind. Every time you find yourself following a new thought, watch it go by—don't push it away, just observe it—then return to your present moment of silence. You can meditate any time of day—for example, early in the morning, between

meetings, or before bed. Try different times and places to see what works best for you.

To learn more about mindfulness and meditation, buy a book on it or attend a meditation class. If you want to learn more in person, there are meditation centers across the country where you can discover the practice of meditation and mindfulness in a professional environment.

There are also many apps that will guide you through meditation. Some of my personal favorites are Oprah and Deepak Chopra's jointly host guided app, Oprah & Deepak 21-Day Meditation Experience, and Headspace, a mobile meditation app that's been downloaded more than 11 million times.

Whatever process works best for you, finding time to clear your thoughts is the most hygge way you can treat your mind and soul.

Reading

It may sound simple, but reading is one of the most hygge things you can do for yourself regularly. Reading quiets our minds and lets us escape the stressors and concerns of our daily lives. Finding joy in reading and taking time to enjoy a new book—whether it's a sci-fi novel, a collection of poetry, or a biography of someone you idolize—is an incredibly hygge activity that you can enjoy almost anywhere, anytime. Enjoying that new bestseller on the beach during a vacation takes your pleasure to a new level. Commuting on the train with a thrilling story stops your mind from worrying about that scary email sitting in your inbox at work. Tucking yourself under the covers with a pop-culture essay before bed can help you fall asleep faster. Each of these simple activities can be all the more hygge if you pull out a book and let your mind escape to a new, fascinating world.

In the summer, pack water and snacks, and lie out on a blanket in the park or at the beach to read in the sun. In the evening, mix up your winding down time by forgoing TV or Netflix and reading on the couch instead. Light candles, have a cup of hot chocolate or a glass of wine, and enjoy the adventure. If you're lucky enough to have a back-yard or patio, take advantage of it in dry weather, year-round. Bundling up in warm clothes and blankets and reading outside in cold air can be incredibly refreshing. When you've had enough, just return indoors and continue reading by the heater or fireplace.

You can also make reading a hygge experience with others. If you're looking for something new to dive into, visit your local library or bookstore with a friend to discuss your favorite titles, make recommendations to each other, and browse new books you each might love. You can also join or form a local book club with friends, and take turns hosting each other in your homes to discuss your reading over candles, food, and wine. If forming a book club around a novel or lengthier read seems overwhelming instead of fun, consider choosing a short story or long article to discuss. This way, no one feels stressed if they can't finish a longer piece of work in time.

Clothing, Style, and Grooming

Has someone's impeccable style ever instantly captured your attention? Did their look feel effortless, made up of uncomplicated yet also unexpected pieces, and make you want to run home to recreate it for yourself right away? That's Danish style in a nutshell—effortless, comfortable, and utterly hygge.

When applying a hygge mind-set to your own style of dress, remember that comfort is key. This doesn't mean you should wear pajamas or sweatpants all day, but that you should feel great in the clothes you wear. Approach your personal style by first considering which clothes and styles make you feel amazing. Do certain shades bring out the color of your eyes? Do suits make you feel confident? Which styles highlight your best physical features? By thinking through what makes you feel great and wearing it often, you can become the person with the style that you've always admired.

Many Danes have a classic, minimalistic sense of dress that doesn't go in and out of style. While everyone has a unique take, here are a few key trends you'll see throughout Scandinavia that can give your own style a hygge update.

Comfortable Shoes. If your feet are comfortable and happy, then you're well on your way to a hygge state of mind. If sneakers aren't your thing, try loafers, boots, or sandals. There's no need to sacrifice comfort for style. And not worrying that your feet will hurt at the end of a long day or a fun evening of dancing is always in style!

Dressing for the Weather. The best way to approach dressing with a hygge mentality is to dress for the season. Danes live by the mantra, "there's no such thing as bad weather, only bad clothes." In warmer months, look for dresses, tops, and bottoms in breathable, natural fabrics—like cotton, linen, and silk. In cooler months, layering is crucial. Tights, thermals, oversized sweaters, and sturdy boots can make even your warm-weather staples winter-ready. Also, a well-cut coat in a

neutral color like black, beige, or gray can last many years, will never go out of style, and will keep you warm and cozy all winter long.

Love it or Leave it. When trying on new clothes, it's important to remember that you'll never love something more than you do in the dressing room. So if it doesn't make you feel amazing and put a big smile on your face right then, don't buy it—no matter how deeply it's discounted or how much you thought you wanted it when you walked into the store.

The Right Fit. Finding your perfect size or having clothing tailored to fit can help you feel comfortable and hygge in any type of clothing. If it feels great on your skin and makes you lift your head higher when you catch a glimpse of yourself in the mirror, then you should wear it—period.

Eating

Next to lighting candles, there's nothing more inherently hygge than preparing and eating delicious food. Sharing food with others, dining at home, and incorporating seasonal ingredients are key aspects to living a more hyggelig life in your kitchen and beyond.

Eating at Home. The most hygge way to have a meal is to prepare and enjoy it in the comfort of your home. For example, whenever someone asks what restaurants in Copenhagen I recommend, my mind draws a blank. I think I ate 99 percent of the meals I had over the years at someone's home. After all, the ritual of cooking can be incredibly relaxing and fun, and it allows you to have complete control over the ingredients, timing, and atmosphere of your meal. If you don't enjoy cooking, then start small. Meal-prep delivery services like Blue Apron or HelloFresh send simple recipes and ingredients to your doorstep so you can prepare gourmet meals at home quickly and easily. Give one a try, and see if you enjoy the process. Or, if you have a friend, roommate, or partner who enjoys cooking more than you do, offer to pitch in for ingredients in exchange for a cooking lesson or two (or just wash the dishes in exchange).

Seasonality. From asparagus in spring and perfect new potatoes in the summer, to Christmas beer during the holidays, Danes make seasonal ingredients the stars of their meals. Incorporating seasonality into your cooking can be incredibly hygge, especially if you shop for your ingredients in local farmers' markets or produce stands. By following the seasons of local produce, you'll start to notice when apples are the crispest, berries are the sweetest, and tomatoes are the brightest. Sourcing ingredients at their peak will make your shopping—and dining—experience all the more delicious.

HYGGE AND CAKE

Cakes, pastries, and sweets are wonderful, and they're important parts of living a hygge life. Enjoying such treats in moderation can make even the most regular of days feel special and celebratory—which is rigtig hyggelig indeed!

On the weekends, Danes delight in sharing sweet pastries, breads, and coffee in the morning, just as Americans enjoy pancakes, avocado toast, and eggs during brunch. It's incredibly hyggelig to wake up early, visit the local bakery, and choose a few of your favorite pastries to share with friends or loved ones. (The sweet pastries that we call "danishes" in the United States are in fact very popular in Denmark, but over there they call them wienerbrød, or Vienna bread.)

Taking a hygge approach to sweets and cakes means eating and sharing them solely because it makes you feel good (but not overindulging). There's no need to only have cake around specific holidays or celebrations—instead, enjoy them here and there on unexpected occasions, when the mood strikes. For example, you could brighten up a cloudy day by making a whimsical straw-berry shortcake for your friends, or surprise your family with a rich chocolate cake after dinner on a random Monday evening when everyone's had a long day.

Enjoying treats occasionally and partaking in their fun, rather than avoiding them entirely or just waiting for predictable occasions, is the hygge way to have your cake and eat it, too.

Setting the Scene. Taking time to enjoy meals and make them special starts with setting a hygge-stemning, or hygge mood. Light a few candles and turn on your favorite playlist, old record, or podcast. Choose a recipe or ingredients that you love. Even if you're dining alone, take care in setting out your meal. Use nice dishes and napkins—even if you ultimately want to eat dinner on the couch. Instead of thinking of mealtime as another task you need to do in a day, give yourself time to enjoy the experience of preparing food and nourishing your body.

Sharing Food with Others. When you enter someone's home or office in Denmark, one of the first things they will ask is, "Have you eaten?" or "Can I get you something?" Sharing food with others is truly hygge at its finest. Next time you make plans with friends, suggest cooking dinner together. You can share the cost of ingredients, bring a bottle of wine, or pitch in on the cleaning—whatever it takes to come together over the preparation and enjoyment of a good meal.

Ultimately, hygge dining is all about enjoying the experience of preparing food for yourself and others, and savoring the food you eat. Eating a mix of nourishing and comforting foods in moderation will make you both happier and healthier—and feel hyggelig, too.

Exercise

While exercise may not be at the forefront of your mind when you think of hygge, it is an important part of a healthy, balanced life, and it can help you de-stress and relax.

Do Something You Love. Finding a workout routine you truly enjoy is the best way to make exercising more hyggelig. If you're not sure what kind of activity you'll like, then take time to try out different classes, venues, and programs. If you love being outside, then running, biking, or joining an outdoor sports league might be the best choice for you. If you love music and rhythm, try signing up for dance or spin classes to get your body moving to the beat. If you love the water, find a local pool, lake, or beach you can visit regularly to make swimming a part of your routine.

It's the Little Things. If you already have a routine you enjoy, you can easily incorporate hygge into your already active life. Instead of the usual vinyasa yoga, try attending a candlelit yoga class, or use essential oils at home while practicing yoga, stretching, or meditating to elevate your experience and make it even more special. Next time you go on a run or power walk, invite a friend. This way, you won't even notice how many steps you accumulate while you're laughing and catching up. And, of course, if you have a dog, be sure to treat them (and yourself) to long walks and playdates often.

Join a Community. You can also make your workout routine more hygge by making it a group activity. Joining a fitness community or exercising with others gives you the opportunity to be a part of a team, make new friends, and experience togetherness. When you're spending time with others and enjoying yourself—on intramural sport teams or in workout classes—exercising won't feel like a chore, but something to look forward to.

Make it a Routine. One of the most hygge ways to exercise is to make it part of your daily life. If you are lucky enough to have the opportunity to commute to work by bike or on foot, then take advantage of it. Getting your blood flowing and breathing fresh air at the start and end of your day can help put you in a more hygge state of mind. If your workplace is too far away to walk or bike there, consider getting off the train one stop early, parking a bit farther away from your office than usual, or walking part or all of the way home.

Mix Things Up. If you get bored easily by one activity, vary your workouts so you're always trying something different. Ease into your week with a calming yoga class, perk yourself up on Wednesday with a fast spin class, and then kick-start the weekend with a run outside. Regularly switching up your workout may be the best way to help you stay excited and motivated.

Above all else, listen to your body and engage in activities you look forward to. And remember that after a great workout, relaxing at home will feel all the more hyggeligt.

Embodying Hygge

By making simple changes to your daily activities and routine, you can incorporate hygge into all aspects of your personal and internal life. You don't need to apply every concept at once. Start small with the thing that's most important to you, and build from there. A hygge mind-set doesn't need to be built in a day, but you're sure to start feeling its positive effects each time you put one of these activities into practice.

Chapter Three

Home

Hygge on the Homefront

Imagine returning home in the middle of winter after a long commute and an even longer day of work. You peel off your many layers and slide into soft, cozy loungewear. The heater or fireplace hums as you raise the temperature. As you settle into your favorite chair, your dog curls up at your feet. The light is soft and flickering, and you can hear the cold wind faintly otutside your windows. You lift the needle on your record player, and the notes of your favorite song waft through the air. Your cheeks tingle as you warm up from the inside out.

This is hygge at its finest.

Home is where the concept of hygge truly shines, and once you've begun applying a hygge mind-set to your life, your living space is a great place to create small changes that can make all the difference. In this chapter, we'll discuss several aspects of a hygge home including lighting, pets, and to how to get a hygge night's sleep.

After all, home is important. It's where we begin and end each day, where we grow our families, take time for ourselves, and go to unwind after work or play. It's where we feed ourselves and others. It's where we sleep and allow our bodies to rest before beginning a new day. Even though home may look different to each of us, by taking steps to make it more hyggelig, we can increase our overall sense of peace, calm, and joy—no matter where we live.

At the end of the day, turning the key in the lock and entering your home should be an experience you look forward to, so taking steps to increase the hygge feeling in your home can help you feel this way.

The Energy of a Space

When was the last time you walked into a room that just made you feel . . . off? Though we don't always realize it, the feel of a space can make an immense impact on our mood. When you feel negative energy, it can change your entire experience—especially if that space is your home.

Luckily, you can do many things to increase the positive energy in your space. First, we'll focus on the feeling of the space. Take a moment to think:

- What do you love?

- What helps you relax?

- What brings you peace and joy?

In your home, you should be surrounded by things that evoke feelings of love, relaxation, peace, and joy. The goal is to make your space feel uniquely you, so that every time you walk in the door, you instantly feel at ease. This is an important step toward hjemmehygge (home hygge).

If you're at home as you read this, take a look around you. What about your home makes you happy and calm? Does anything in it make you feel the opposite of those things? Jot your answers down on paper.

If you love color, for example, you'll likely want to add pops of it to your space. You can do this in small ways—through accent pillows, bright artwork, cheerful furniture, or even a painted wall or doorway. For example, I went with a bright yellow couch for my pop of color. A bold, somewhat strange choice, yes, but now it's my favorite part of my home. It's not only the first thing people notice and comment on when they walk through the door, but I also know they can actually feel *me* emanating from the bright, warm color.

If you love to read, you may want bookshelves throughout your home. Organizing books in beautiful ways and making them a focal point of your living space will give you more opportunities to admire and appreciate them—and it will also frequently remind you to pick one out, open it up, and relax into another world.

At the end of the day, we want our homes to feel familiar, warm, and inviting. We want our guests to feel welcome and comfortable in our space. If we take time to notice the energy of our homes and make adjustments to increase positive feelings, we can experience more hygge and joy each day.

Lighting

Lighting is one of the easiest ways to achieve hjemmehygge (home hygge). After all, light can transform almost anything, from how colors appear to how well we sleep. This is especially true in colder months, when daylight is scarce. Taking time to adjust the lighting of your home can make all the difference.

Using light to make your home more hygge is simple—and small changes can make a big impact. Here are a few ways you can make your home even more cozy, peaceful, and welcoming.

Candles. These are one of the most important elements of hjemmehygge. When incorporating candles into your decor, look for smaller styles in natural colors like white and beige. Also look for unscented ones—strong smells, even pleasant ones, can be overwhelming or distracting, especially if you're cooking dinner or serving food. There are many ways to display candles in your home. Tea candles are small, short lights that are often used for just one evening. They are perfect for creating a hyggelig atmosphere without getting in the way of guests, food, décor, or entertainment. You can display long candles on dining tables and mantles for special or more formal occasions or holidays. Most importantly: use your candles! Don't save them for guests or special occasions. Allow yourself to enjoy them and relax in the morning, noon, or evening. Just don't forget to blow them out before leaving the room or going to sleep.

A WORD ON CANDLES

Danes love candles—on average, each person burns around 13 pounds of them per year, which is more than people do in any other European country. They light candles year-round: outside in summer to brighten up dinner with friends in the garden, or to warm up the atmosphere of their homes in winter. They light candles for celebrations like birthdays and Christmas, but also when they are home alone or dining with only their families. Even offices light candles throughout the day—talk about a hyggelig work environment!

Candles aren't just beloved by Danes, however. They are also an integral part of many spiritual ceremonies the world over. Some people believe that the soft illumination of candlelight can touch your soul, and some find that candlelight helps achieve a meditative state. Candles have also been found to help our bodies relax: when our brain registers a candle's soft glow, our mind's associations with it make us feel more relaxed and at ease. Therefore, it's not surprising that many consider candles to be the embodiment of hygge.

Vary Your Lighting. Lighting should be, above all else, adjustable. Incorporating different lighting elements throughout your home allows you to change the space and mood with just the flick of a switch. In addition to installed lighting, like ceiling bulbs or sconces, consider adding table and floor lamps throughout your space, particularly in areas that could use their own brightness—for example, a reading nook, the dining table, or your bedside. To change the mood, add some candlelight, and turn certain lights off or on. Experiment by adjusting the warmth and brightness of your space according to the time of day or your activity.

Think Outside the Box. Lighting doesn't need to come from lamps or installations alone. To add a magical hygge element to your home, consider draping fairy or Christmas tree lights around a doorway, staircase railing, or window frame. Neon or marquee signs with lights that can be switched on and off are also cozy, creative ways to add light and design to your space.

Natural Light. Of course, the best way to brighten your space is with sunlight. If you're lucky enough to have large windows, be sure to take advantage of them. Hang translucent or light (white) curtains that can be opened or closed depending on the time of day. Open windows bring a natural lightness and airiness to your space that feels very hyggeligt. If you don't have much natural light in your apartment, consider sun lamps or lightbulbs that mimic daylight to make your space a bit less dim.

Décor

Hygge homes are relaxed and personal. Instead of feeling precious or formal, they welcome you to sit down and make yourself comfortable. Hygge homes do not "save the good china for the queen." In fact, they likely don't have any good china—just beautiful dishware that is beloved and used often. Are you ready for a hygge redesign? Here are a few ideas to get you started.

Decoration. Like the rest of your hygge home, decoration should be personal, welcoming, and even functional. Books are innately hyggelig, so if you have a collection you love, be sure to display it. Coffee table books look great in the living room and invite conversation among guests, and smaller books can be organized on shelves along with personal photos and other treasures. Plants are another hyggelig way to decorate. The freshness and natural beauty they bring to a room can make all the difference.

Furniture. How your furniture feels is important for a hygge home. Pieces that marry comfort and function will help you and any guests relax. Look for couches that are cozy and soft, but easy to clean. Incorporate poufs or ottomans in your living room that invite you to put your feet up at the end of the day. Add a bench by the front door so you can easily change in and out of shoes. Include barstools in your kitchen so you can spend time with family or guests while cooking. Basically, look for furniture that makes your space more friendly and inviting.

Pillows. A good dose of pillows is an important ingredient in any hygge home. They not only add actual comfort, but having them readily available also makes getting into a hygge state of mind easy. When buying pillows, look for varying sizes to accent your couch, chairs, and bedroom. They should be soft and functional—think velvet, woven cloth, or cotton, but nothing overly designed or accented. To mix things up seasonally, you can look for pillow covers in different colors and materials that you can swap in and out. Just by changing a the look of a few pillows, you can update a space

quickly and effectively. Finally, if you have firm dining or garden chairs, keep cushions on hand to give them a more hygge feel when in they're use.

Blankets. Similar to pillows, blankets bring comfort and warmth to your home. They should be readily available and enjoyed often. Look for styles that are comfortable, soft, and functional, in varying thicknesses. Leave light blankets out in summer for when the AC gets too cool or for grabbing on the way to a picnic. When the weather turns cold, keep thicker blankets close by. In addition to their coziness, blankets are a great way to decorate. Look for colors and designs that you love and that mix well with your aesthetic. Drape one over the back of your couch, fold and hang several on a ladder against the wall, or store them in a large basket near your seating area for easy access.

Fireplace. Fireplaces are wonderfully hygge, so if you're lucky enough to have one, be sure to use it. If you don't have a fireplace built into your home, there are a few alternatives that can mimic the feeling of one. Gas fireplaces are relatively easy to install if you own your home. When you turn them on, many are hard to distinguish from an actual fire with logs. Electric heaters can also create the feeling of being warmed by a fire. The cheapest and easiest way to achieve the fireplace effect (and one which can double as a joke or conversation starter) is to play a video of a fire crackling on your TV. You can this on Netflix and a few other apps.

Feng Shui

Feng shui is an ancient Chinese practice used to increase the flow of positive energy in the home. It became popular in the United States in the 1960s and 1970s. Traditional feng shui (which translates to "wind and water") focuses on the importance of the five natural elements in Chinese culture—water, fire, wood, metal, and earth—and a balance of yin and yang (feminine and masculine energies, respectively). Feng shui also takes into account the directional areas of your home—north, south, east, and west.

Westerners have adapted traditional practices of feng shui to their own cultures, and while traditional and modern feng shui may differ, at the core they both aim to bring more positive energy to the home and to life in general—very hyggelig, don't you think?

While there are many dedicated resources to help you apply feng shui principles to your home, here are a few that can make your home feel more hyggeligt.

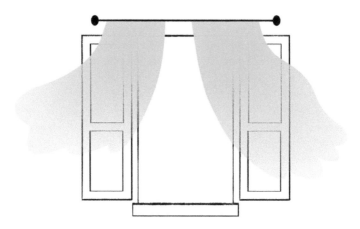

Light and Air. Positive energy goes hand in hand with having a good flow of air and light in your home. Keep windows open whenever possible to let fresh air in and stale air out, and open curtains to let sunlight in. Air purifiers, humidifiers, and houseplants can also help increase the quality of the air around you.

Mirrors. When placed in the right locations, mirrors can bring a wonderful energy into your home. They expand your space by reflecting their surroundings, making even the smallest room feel more comfortable. They also naturally reflect and bounce light, which can help brighten your home. Feng shui recommends placing mirrors in the north, east, and southeast areas of your home, and suggests that you avoid placing mirrors above your bed and your main door, or on a southern wall.

Color. In feng shui, colors represent each of the five elements—water, fire, wood, metal, and earth. While Scandinavian style generally revolves around a lighter, more neutral palette—I can't think of a single Danish home I've been to that had walls painted any color other than white—adding accents of color throughout your home can increase your overall joy and enjoyment of the space. Using light colors—earth, metal—to decorate your home can give it a bright, airy quality that feels hyggeligt. A light, neutral base also allows you to be more playful with your artwork or decorations, so don't be afraid to incorporate a pop of color here and there—red for fire, green for wood, blue for water, etc. Follow feng shui guidelines to place these colors in the most beneficial areas throughout your home, so you can feel the greatest increase in positive energy.

Minimalism

From *The Life-Changing Magic of Tidying Up*, by Marie Kondō, to *The Art of Swedish Death Cleaning*, by Margareta Magnusson, minimalism is a trend in interior design and modern lifestyles. This makes sense as millennials trend toward spending money on experiences rather than things—72 percent, in fact, according to a recent study CNBC reported by Harris Group Inc.

Luckily, this trend is also hyggelig. By taking a minimalist approach to possessions and decluttering your home, you can ensure that your home contains only the things that bring you comfort and joy. Minimalism also enables you to better appreciate what you own, instead of filling your home with things that aren't meaningful to you. Here are a few simple ways minimalism can increase your hjemmehygge.

Take Inventory. Go through your home and take stock of what you have. Do you have duplicates of things you just need one of? Do you have things that no longer work or fit? Do you have things you no longer have a use for in your daily life? How

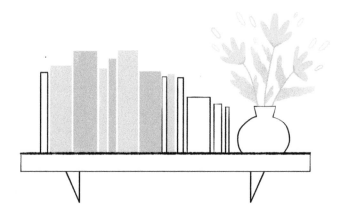

about items that are seasonal only? Sort your possessions accordingly into different piles. You can start with these four: donate, keep, store, and throw away. When your throw-away and donate piles start getting large, take them out of your home. Keep your storage pile organized in closets, drawers, or labeled organizers for easy access when you need these items again. Finally, return the things in your keep pile to their rightful places in a clean, orderly fashion. You can go room by room or section by section to keep from getting overwhelmed. For example, in your kitchen, you can start with your pantry and then move to your dishes, cleaning supplies, and so on.

A Place for Everything. When you've taken inventory of your possessions and cleared out things you don't need or no longer enjoy, take time to find the right places for your remaining items. Feel free to hide things you don't use all the time in organizers, drawers, boxes, and so forth—just keep them clean and organized for easy access.

Seasonal Refreshes. Every six months or so, before the start of hot weather or cold weather, set aside time to refresh your space. Change out your winter wardrobe and blankets for lighter items in the summer, and then, when the weather gets cold again, put away your summer items. This way, everything that's out and available is useful and practical. While you do this transition, take stock of your things. Do they still fit? Do you love them? Are they worn out or still in style? If you don't pull them out or wear them during the season they're meant for, then it's time to give them away.

Think Before You Buy. Once everything in your home has a place and a purpose, be extra conscious about which new items you introduce. Think in terms of quality over quantity and how much you will use each item. This can ensure that only things you love and use will take up space in your home.

Textures and Materials

When building a hygge atmosphere in your home, take time to add textures and materials that bring you comfort and enhance relaxation. There are many ways to do this that keep it simple. You don't need to buy all new furniture to be extra plush or your floors or carpet to achieve a hygge feeling. Consider these ways to create a more hyggelig atmosphere:

Knits. Knitted pieces feel relaxing, comfortable, and homemade. Add a knitted blanket to your couch or bed—if you're feeling bold, try a style woven with extra-thick yarn—or add knitted accents like throw pillows or knitted stool covers.

Natural Materials. Natural textures are more hygge than their synthetic counterparts. Elements like wood, stone, ceramic, and marble feel grounded and foundational—much more than plastic or metals. Incorporate them into your home in furniture, dishware, and decoration. Look for blankets, pillows, and accents in natural fibers such as cashmere, linen, silk, and wool to establish a feeling of hygge.

Rugs. Most homes in Denmark have hardwood floors, not carpeting. To achieve a hygge feeling beneath your feet, no matter what kind of floors you have, look for thick rugs of different shapes and sizes. You can even layer rugs on top of each other to add more thickness in certain areas and play with color and design. Mixing rugs throughout your home can give each room a different feeling and texture.

Sheepskin. One of the most hygge textures you'll see throughout Scandinavian design is sheepskin—whether thrown over the back of a chair or at the foot of the bed. They can give any space in your home a cozier feel, and they come in faux versions if you'd like to avoid animal products.

Your Bedroom

Your bedroom is one of the most important places where you can add hygge to your home. After all, we spend a lot of our time in bed—according to a Gallup poll reported by NPR, the average American sleeps 6.8 hours a night, which is nearly 2,500 hours a year. While this seems like a lot over time, more than 40 percent of Americans actually think they'd feel better if they were able to sleep more.

Taking time to bring a feeling of hygge into your bed and bedroom can help you get to sleep faster, so you can wake up refreshed and ready to start your day. Here are a few tips for a more hyggelig bedroom.

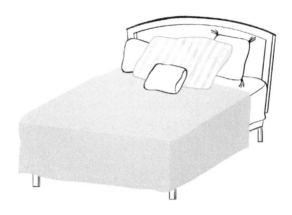

Bedding. One of the first things I noticed when I moved to Denmark was that top sheets don't seem to exist. Instead of multiple layers—top sheets, blankets, and comforters—Danes almost always sleep with just a fitted sheet and a single duvet. You can get duvets in different thicknesses—lightweight for summer and heavier for winter—and swap their covers just as you do with pillowcases. In Denmark, even couples who share beds often have separate duvets—which means no worrying about hogging the blanket. Look for fitted sheets and duvet covers made of natural materials like cotton or linen, which will feel cooler on your body as you settle in for a hygge night's sleep.

Fresh Air. Fresh air is important throughout your house, and is especially important in your bedroom. An Eindhoven University of Technology study reported by Sci News compared people sleeping in different environments, and found that those who slept with open windows and doors slept better than those in sealed rooms. It found that less carbon dioxide in the open rooms led to fewer awakenings during the night and increased sleep depth.

Light and Sound. Bright lights can be the opposite of hygge—especially when you're trying to wind down for sleep. Consider avoiding overhead lighting or adding dimmers to your bedroom lights so you can reduce the brightness as you get ready for bed. Bedside lamps with warm light are also a good alternative. When you're ready to sleep, consider playing white noise, ocean sounds, or even soft yoga music as you drift off. This can help clear your mind and keep you in a hygge mind-set.

Pets

When I tell people I have a dog, I always look forward to their reaction. Nine times out of ten, their faces light up and their smiles widen. Quite simply, animals make people happy, and having pets in your home can infuse every single day with a feeling of hygge. I adopted my dog, Bennett—a Pomeranian mix with dark brown fur and eyes—two years after moving to New York. I was living in a small studio apartment with no light, and as soon as he arrived, he brightened up my home more than I could have ever imagined. Four years later, sitting on the sofa with him curled up next to me, I can't imagine feeling at home without him.

We all know that pets can be loving, cuddly additions to our lives, but there are many additional health and wellness benefits to having them. A University of Buffalo study reported by *Woman's Day* found that people feel less stress when they're with their pets than they do when they're with family or close friends. Many hospitals and rehabilitation centers also use pets to help treat people's anxiety, improve their social interactions, calm impulsive aggression, and more. Simply petting animals has

been linked to lower blood pressure and increased energy. Additionally, a Harvard Medical School study found that dog owners tend to have better heart health, including lower blood pressure and cholesterol.

Pets can also give you a sense of purpose and responsibility at home, which can bring a lot of satisfaction and joy. After all, every time you get home, they'll be so happy to see you that you won't be able to keep from smiling. Pets are wonderful hygge welcome committees 24 hours a day, seven days a week.

Animals can also increase your feeling of hygge by helping you unplug and de-stress, whether by curling up with you on the couch or playing games with you inside or outdoors. They bring positive energy into your home, whether they're finding overwhelming joy in something unexpected—like dust particles in the air or a stray piece of ribbon—or showing affection by snuggling next to you or licking your face or hands. Pets can also give your guests a more hyggelig experience by welcoming them into your home with kisses and love.

A Hygge Home

You probably spend a significant portion of your time at home and much of your income on your rent or mortgage, so taking steps to make sure your living space feels like a welcome, comforting sanctuary is an important part of living a more hygge life. When you create a sense of hjemmehygge, your home can become an oasis that brings you more joy every day.

Chapter Four

Family & Community

Getting Social with Hygge

Spending quality social time with others is not just an incredibly hygge experience, it's a well-documented part of living a longer, healthier life. Social interaction can decrease depression and raise feelings of well-being. It can also help relieve physical pain. A *Medical News Today* study found that just the touch of a romantic partner can help lessen one's experience of pain. Additionally, according to a study by *The Lancet Neurology*, those who engage in social activities are at a lower risk for dementia than those who are more isolated.

Whether you socialize in a group or prefer one-on-one hangouts, the important thing is to spend time with others. Hygge social interactions can be with family members and close friends, or with people you're still getting to know, like colleagues and neighbors.

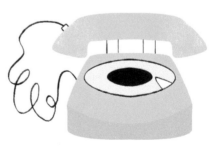

Having people you see often is wonderful. These relationships are important as you build a hygge community around you. However, in a truly balanced hyggelig life, the relationships you have with friends and family you don't see as often or feel as close to are equally meaningful. Calling unexpectedly just to say hello, sending letters or cards, and remembering birthdays can go a long way toward lasting relation-ships, no matter how often you're in the same city or room.

No matter who you're spending time with, it's important to create a warm, inviting atmosphere. While each person may have a different idea of what that looks like, sharing a common hyggestund (hygge experience) can help everyone feel more hyggelige and happy together.

A few of the most important aspects of having a hygge family and community are spending qual-ity time together, making meaningful connections, sharing meals, and incorporating traditions. In this chapter, we'll discuss each of these, along with how to infuse hygge into your holidays and conversations.

Meals with Others

This past summer, I stopped by the Copenhagen Cooking & Food Festival and sat down with a group of Danes over plates of fresh cheese and glasses of cider. When hygge came up, I asked the man sitting next to me what came to mind when he thought of the concept.

"Sharing food with others," he said.

Looking around the table at the group of people I'd just met, who were laughing and literally breaking bread together in the summer sun, I smiled and nodded in agreement.

Next to lighting candles, sharing food with others truly is one of the most hygge experiences you can have (but feel free to light candles during your meal for an even more hyggelig atmosphere). The food doesn't need to be fancy, the number of guests can be small or large, and you can eat just about anywhere—at the dining table, gathered in the park, on cushions around the living room, or even around a picnic table at a food festival.

Years ago, when I moved to Copenhagen for university, I lived in a dormitory with 15 other students. Though we all had our own rooms—whether

a single or a double—we shared a large kitchen and common area. Every week, someone would sign up for *madklub* (dinner club) duty and cook dinner for the entire group. We'd all pitch in money for ingredients, help set the table and clean the kitchen, and then we would gather around to eat the same meal at the same time. We were all from different places, studying different subjects, and leading mostly separate lives, but once a week we came together like family to share food and stories. As fall turned to winter, these meals brought us closer, and when I think back, those memories stand out to me more than anything else during my time living there.

You don't have to host lots of guests or go out of your way to experience a hygge meal with friends. To pull together group experiences more often, try letting go of the stress and anxiety around planning. It doesn't have to be perfect. Text friends to invite them over for dinner or to go out to eat just a few days ahead of time—or even the same day—and don't worry about how many or how few people can join. On the day you meet up, you can order takeout, meet at a favorite restaurant, pack a picnic lunch to take to the park, or hold a potluck where everyone brings a different element of the meal to share. If you feel like cooking, then preparing a simple, warm recipe that can be served family style, such as soup, chili, or pasta, can be incredibly hyggelig. Allow guests to serve themselves, add a few lit candles, and have ice cream (which requires no prep!) for dessert. Voila! You've created a perfectly hygge meal with friends.

It may sound simple—because it is!—but the most important thing is to come together for great food and conversation. Who knows, maybe soon you'll even start a dinner club of your own.

Time with Friends and Family

When you build a supportive, loving community around you, a confidence and sense of ease sets in because you know you have people in your life who will accept and support you when you need it most.

There are many ways you can apply a hygge mind-set to your time with family and friends, and make your social experiences with them even more meaningful. We've looked at how sharing food with others is a hygge activity that provides the opportunity for worthwhile conversation and connection. Inviting friends and family into your home can also help you feel more connected to them, and the openness of this experience can bring you closer together.

Another way to spend quality hygge time with friends or family is through common activities. Take a class together, go on a long walk or run together, or join the same social club or religious group. Volunteer for an organization that's meaningful to both of you, such as an animal welfare group or a community garden or kitchen. Taking time to give back to society together can strengthen your relationship and make you both feel good.

Spending meaningful time with others doesn't always have to be in person—sometimes you can just pick up the phone and reach out. Catching up with friends or family while commuting, walking your dog, or cleaning up at home can be a hyggelig way to keep in touch while being productive. (Just don't try to do too many things at once, or you may be distracted from the conversation.) Even a short call to your loved ones when you're taking a 10-minute walk to the grocery store can be a highlight for both of you. Just letting your relative know, "I only have 10 minutes to talk, but I wanted

to see how you're doing," can help bring a smile to both of your faces and deepen your kinship. Don't feel as though you have to wait until you have an extended period of free time to catch up—sometimes just a "Hello, I'm thinking of you" text can go a long way. FaceTime and Skype are also great ways to stay connected. Even when you're seeing one another through a screen, you're still smiling, making eye contact, and enjoying each other's company.

Playing Host

These days, it's easy to become friends with someone without ever seeing the inside of their home. We meet at new restaurants, catch afternoon movies, and say cheers at happy hours long before we see what each other's living rooms look like or discover how we organize our bookshelves (by color? by size? by genre?).

After all, we live in an age that values experiences. Between dining out, weekend getaways, and general FOMO (fear of missing out), it's easy to forget the hygge experiences we can share with our friends right in the comfort of our own homes.

We forgo this experience for many reasons. For example, we don't want to be judged, we don't think we can cook, or we think our homes are too small or too messy. But playing host(ess) doesn't need to be intimidating; it can be something to look forward to. Gone are the pressed aprons and complicated roasts of the past. Today, all you need is a warm smile, a cool playlist, and hot appetizers (you can never go wrong with something from Trader Joe's). I promise that your guests will be just as happy to be there as you are to have them.

YOUR CHOSEN FAMILY

To each of us, the word *family* can mean something different. We may have lost parents or siblings. Our parents may have divorced. We may not know both of our parents or we may be estranged from them. We may have stepparents or blended families. We may be only children or have many brothers and sisters.

No matter what family looks like to you, you can always surround yourself with hyggelige friends (hyggespreders) and relationships that feel like family. It's been said that "friends are the family you choose," and I believe this to be true.

We all have the opportunity to build a chosen family. By deciding to surround yourself with people who share your values, lift you higher, or make you laugh until you cry, you are taking an important step toward infusing more hygge in your life. Fostering connections with your chosen family is a hygge experience, and you can apply the values in this chapter to your relationships with blood relatives, friends, friends' relatives, or even colleagues and neighbors.

continued →

To nurture relationships with your chosen family, simply treat them just like family. Call them out of the blue, invite them over often, and even invite yourself over to their house. Take them to dinner on their birthdays and celebrate major holidays together. Offer to care for each other's pets or children, and bring them food when they're not feeling well. These gestures will strengthen your support network and bring hygge and joy to your life.

Even the act of preparing to welcome friends into your home can be a hygge experience. Take time to find a recipe that excites you and that you know your guests will love—the simpler, the better. (For example, have you tried cacio e pepe? It's spaghetti with cheese and pepper—couldn't be simpler!) Clean your home until it shines, even in those places you overlook when you know you're the only one who will notice. Buy your favorite flowers on your way home from work. Strike a match to light the candles you've been saving for a special occasion. Stop to smile and take pride in the home you've created for yourself.

If you're new to hosting, you can always start small. Invite just one or two close friends. Time the invitation around the return of your favorite TV show or the celebration of someone's promotion at work. Ask your guests to bring drinks to share. Order pizza from your favorite restaurant (bonus points if you sprinkle torn basil leaves on top or set out freshly grated Parmesan). Let Pandora or Spotify set the tone. Eat around the table or have an indoor picnic; the more pillows, the better. Let

your friends help with the dishes when they ask, and send them home with leftovers.

Most importantly, enjoy yourself. Because there's nothing quite like seeing your friends make themselves at home in the space you call home.

Incorporating Traditions

One of my favorite things about Denmark is its many hygge traditions and customs—especially around the holidays. From Christmas and New Year's to Easter and Midsummer's Eve, each new season is accompanied by wonderful traditions that embody hygge in every way.

In Denmark, Christmas is undeniably the most hygge time of year. That said, the Danes are not especially religious, so the holiday brings with it many secular traditions that everyone can enjoy, no matter their faith. Throughout the season, everyone attends numerous hygge julefrokosts, or Christmas lunches. You may have a julefrokost with your friends, then with your family, then with your colleagues, then with a friend's friend, and so on, each time enjoying traditional dishes like crispy roast pig, herring, and risalamande for dessert. (Risalamande is a traditional rice pudding that is served with cherry sauce and in which one whole almond is hidden; the lucky winner who finds the almond takes home a prize.)

As everyone gathers inside to enjoy great food, say "*skål!*" (cheers), and experience the joy of the season by candlelight, it's easy to see why Christmas in Denmark is rigtig hyggelig. The extra cheer, time with family and friends, and hygge festivities give you plenty to look forward to during the dreariest months of winter.

But the holidays aren't the only time of year when hygge traditions emerge. Any tradition that allows you to spend time with the people you love, make lasting memories, and find more gratitude is inherently hygge.

Which traditions do your family or friends celebrate throughout the year? Do you play Monopoly on New Year's Eve? Or barbeque with friends every Fourth of July? Do you attend a regular book club or game night with friends? More than likely, you already celebrate hygge traditions year-round, perhaps without even realizing it.

If you want to introduce more traditions into your life and relationships, consider what you love to do. Perhaps you can meet a friend at your favorite diner for a late-night dinner once a year, join the same group of friends for a regular brunch date, or even call your mom on FaceTime every Sunday. These seemingly small traditions add up quickly, bringing joy, value, and positivity to your life. And, if nothing else, consider hosting a julefrokost and starting a new hygge tradition you'll carry on for years to come.

Thanksgiving

I grew up in Oregon with two chefs for parents, so Thanksgiving was the holiday I looked forward to the most. My mom would make scones for breakfast while we watched the Macy's Thanksgiving Day Parade on TV, and my dad would begin the complicated process of preparing the turkey with help from my younger brother.

When I first moved to Denmark at 16, people at school warned the international students that the holidays would be the hardest time for us to get through. We'd be past the excitement of living in a new place and would be starting to miss home. Luckily, I didn't have much time to feel sad as the holiday approached, because my new Danish friends and family couldn't wait to celebrate Thanksgiving with me.

During my years in Denmark, I hosted many Thanksgiving dinners with Danish friends and loved when those friends took ownership of my American holiday. It truly made them feel like part of my family. While Thanksgiving is an American holiday, many Danes absolutely love the tradition, since it is the ultimate embodiment of hygge. After all, it combines so many hygge elements into one evening—expressing and feeling gratitude; sharing warm, hearty food with friends and family; spending hours celebrating together, engaging in joyful conversation, lighting candles; setting a beautiful table spread; and so on.

Think about your favorite Thanksgiving traditions. Which ones feel the coziest and make you feel the most grateful? How can you recreate that feeling year-round?

Between my brother and I moving to different states and my parents getting divorced, Thanksgiving celebrations in my family have changed a lot over the years. But the hygge feeling of the day carries on. No matter which city we're in or who hosts dinner, the day is still always filled with gratitude, love, and lots of great food.

Children

Spending time with children can be a wonderful way to experience hygge. After all, kids tend to be friendly and welcoming, find the joy in the little things, love to be playful and carefree, and see the world with fresh, wondrous eyes. To them, every day is one to be enjoyed freely and without anxiety. What's more hyggelig than that?

By sharing quality time with children—whether your own, your family's, or your friends'—you can begin seeing things from their perspective. I promise it will help you to appreciate life through a more innocent lens.

I don't have children of my own yet, but my friend Josefine has a seven-year-old daughter named Angelina who is a joy to be around. When we get together, we'll often visit Central Park for a picnic or a game of Frisbee (she's very good!), order ice cream, and swing as high as we can at the playground—all hygge activities that I might not partake in normally as an adult. Angelina has the biggest heart, widest smile, and most infectious happiness that I can't help but catch whenever I spend time with her. No matter what mood I'm in, she always helps me remember how much light and goodness exists in the world and brings be back to a hygge state of mind.

Just like a day in the park with Angelina, there are many experiences that children can make even more hyggelige. Playing games with them, whether

board games or sports or something more imaginary, can remind you how wonderful it is to just play without worrying about winning or losing. Similarly, creative projects can be all the more fun with children. My friend Signe has two wonderful daughters who keep her constantly on her toes, always dreaming up new artistic endeavors, from designing Barbie outfits to filling coloring books and baking delicious treats.

Kids can help you add hygge to your day-to-day activities, too. Give them a chance to help out in the kitchen or do chores around the house, or let them lead you on morning or nighttime walks in the neighborhood. Not only will it help you teach them valuable life lessons, but it will also allow them remind you how to find joy in even the most mundane of tasks and activities.

Conversation

An important part of having meaningful, quality relationships is communication. How you share with, converse with, and listen to others strongly affects your social interactions. Hyggelige conversations are thoughtful, honest, and open—not tense or argumentative.

Sometimes conversation flows like water, easily and without stopping—especially when you're catching up with a good friend you haven't seen in a while. Other times, especially around people you see all the time, like family or colleagues, you may feel like you've run out of things to say. To avoid this feeling, come prepared. Preparing to be social may sound strange, but having a few questions or talking points at the ready can invigorate otherwise stale conversations and lead to a much stronger connection.

Are you listening to a new, interesting podcast? Tell your friends or family something you learned from it, and ask for their thoughts. Chances are, this will remind them of a fun fact or podcast they'd love to share, too. Asking questions about shared experiences can also be a great conversation starter. For example, a story about something odd or funny that happened during your commute can launch hours of conversation about strange experiences or even what everyone does on their commutes (listen to music, read, sleep, etc.). Sometimes, all it takes to start a conversation is a good question or personal story.

To have the most hyggelige conversations, strive to listen more than you speak. Researchers at Harvard University discovered that people derive the same pleasure talking about themselves as they do enjoying food—so ask as many questions as you answer, if not more. Make eye contact with others as they talk, and be fully present in the moment and with their story. Sometimes, it's easy to let your mind wander—suddenly, you're thinking of something you forgot to do at work, an item you forgot to buy at the grocery store, or how much you have to do tomorrow. If you notice your attention straying, bring it back to the present moment and concentrate on listening intently.

Lastly, because it needs to be said, try not to look at your phone! Unplugging it, placing it facedown in another room, or even leaving your phone at home (gasp!) while spending time with your family and friends can help you foster a more meaningful connection.

Snail Mail

Although today most people prefer to dash off a quick email or text, the art of letter writing continues to be a meaningful and personal way to communicate—especially now that it's so unexpected. Think of the last time you received a kind postcard in the mail from a friend or relative. How did it make you feel? Sending such a note yourself can truly feel just as wonderful—if not more so. By reaching out to friends and family in this traditional yet unexpected way, you are applying the principles of hygge to your relationships through thoughtful action.

If writing a letter seems intimidating, create a manageable goal, such as writing one postcard per month to a family member or friend. Buy a roll of stamps at the post office or corner store so you're prepared when you find time to write. Collect cards and postcards that will suit any occasion. Bookstores, gift shops, and even grocery stores often have affordable, sweet options.

The content of your note can be anything you like—a brief update on your life, a funny thing that reminded you of the recipient, or just a sentence

or two saying that you're thinking of them. The content truly doesn't matter much—the important thing to convey is that you care about them. It also doesn't matter how close or far away they live—you can send a postcard to your next-door neighbor if you'd like. The effect is the same. For example, a friend recently visited me in New York, and when she returned to Los Angeles, I realized she'd left a Polaroid photo behind and that it was the perfect opportunity to send her a surprise note. I wrote a few words on a plain card, thanking her for her visit and friendship, included the photo, and sent it off to her home. Just imagining her smile when she discovered what was inside was well worth the postage.

Another simple way to show someone you care through the mail is by letting someone else do the sending. Sometimes, after discussing a book with a friend or family member, I'll order it for them online. I'll simply send it as a gift with a note attached that says I hope they enjoy it. This is a simple thing you can do with just a few clicks that will surprise and delight someone you care about.

It's amazing how seemingly superficial and small actions such as these can deepen your relationships and bring you more happiness and connection with people.

Sharing Hygge

You can apply the values of hygge we've discussed in this chapter to many different relationships and social interactions. Social relationships permeate every aspect of our lives, and by fostering more hyggelige moments with family and friends, you'll set yourself up to find more happiness every day—and to bring more happiness to others.

Chapter Five

Work & Career

Hygge at Work

Many of us work morning to night, five days a week—or more. We work overtime to seize opportunities, to pursue careers we're passionate about, or simply because we think we need to in order to do our best work and earn our next promotion or raise.

The time we spend on work and the stress that accompanies it can hinder our ability to lead more hyggelige lives—but it doesn't have to. By applying concepts of hygge to our work and career, we can make our workspaces more comfortable and find a better work-life balance.

In chapter 1, we discussed how people often find more gratification when they are working toward goals rather than once they've reached them. So finding ways to increase your satisfaction as you go can improve your mood and increase the likelihood of experiencing hygge each day.

In many ways, applying hygge to your work and career combines hygge concepts from the other aspects of your life that we've already covered. This is because your work and career combine everything we've talked about so far—yourself, your community, and your physical environment—so making simple changes in these areas can make a big impact on your daily happiness.

Unless you work for yourself, you probably have less control over your work environment and career than you do in other parts of your life. Those who work outside of their homes often have offices, colleagues, and desks they have to accept and work productively with, even if they do not particularly like them. In this chapter, we'll explore creative ways to infuse even the most static of work environments with the essence of hygge.

Transforming a Cubicle or Desk

A few years ago, I was working in an open office that was built into an old warehouse. While it had big windows that let in wonderful light, otherwise the space was the opposite of hygge: cold concrete floors and industrial desks as far as the eye could see.

Then my colleague Megan joined our team. Overnight, she transformed her corner desk into a creative's dream. By adding her own gold file organizer, a few lush green plants, chic penholders with brightly colored pens, and clear Lucite accents, she turned her desk into one of the most beautiful, hyggelig workspace I'd ever seen.

However small and sterile your desk may be, you too can make simple changes to give it a hyggelig vibe. Take a cue from Megan and personalize your space; find small items that will make your day-to-day workspace more appealing and creative. Here are a few ideas to get you started.

Make it Feel More Like Home. Incorporate your favorite colors throughout your space. Add a small piece of art to brighten things up. Add a soft-lit lamp to counter harsh fluorescent lighting—choose one with character, like a hand-hewn wooden base and an old-timey bulb that shows the filaments. Hang a cork or magnetic board behind your computer to display notes, mementos, and photos. (This may seem obvious, but it's one of the simplest ways to add a more hyggelig feeling to your desk. Not only will these remind you of the people you love throughout the day, but they will help ensure that you leave work at a reasonable time so you can spend time with them.) Use stylish frames to help your space feel less corporate.

Add Life to Your Desk (Literally). Plants can have an incredible effect on your desk space with minimal effort. Whether you choose one medium-sized leafy green plant or a cluster of small succulents, adding flora can improve the energy of any space.

Swap the Generic Office Tools. While your office may have standard pens and other supplies, bringing your own ensures that you're working with the materials that feel the best to you.

Make Your Desk a Destination. Add a bowl of candy or other small goodies to your desk so everyone knows the best spot to grab a treat, which will help you foster new hyggelige connections.

Atmosphere

In cases where you can't change your physical surroundings, there are still many ways you can get in a hygge mind-set and make your work experience more pleasant.

Have a Mug Handy. It may sound simple, but keeping a beloved mug at work can make you feel much more cozy. Pour yourself hot cups of tea or coffee throughout the day to stay warm and feel more hyggeligt. If your office doesn't provide beverages, bring in your own selection of tea to keep at your desk. If you're a coffee drinker, having a single-use French press is an easy way to brew fresh, delicious coffee any time of day. Bring in a bag of nice coffee grounds and even your favorite creamer to make your coffee routine feel more like the one you have at home.

Hygge in Your Headphones. If you're in an open office or a loud environment, focusing and getting in a creative, productive mood can be hard. Try drowning out the noise with headphones by listening to music that helps you concentrate. Create playlists filled with songs that make you feel peaceful while you work. I personally have trouble focusing while listening to lyrics, so listening to jazz or classical music helps me relax and tune in to whatever I'm working on. Additionally, listening to music before a big presentation or a meeting you're not looking forward to can help you feel more comfortable, relaxed, and prepared.

Take Time to Breathe. With constant deadlines, meetings, and email inboxes that never quite get cleared out, it can be easy to go a whole workday without taking a moment for yourself. Look for opportunities throughout your day when you can breathe and reset. After a meeting, take a few deep breaths before returning to your desk, or raise your arms to stretch when you notice you've tensed up. If possible, go for a walk around the block or climb the stairs instead of taking the elevator. Even small exercises like this can help clear

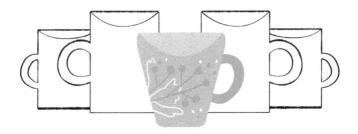

FURRY FRIENDS IN THE OFFICE

Lately, it's become increasingly common for businesses to adopt dog-friendly office policies, especially in the tech and start-up fields. According to a 2017 study published in the *International Journal of Environmental Research and Public Health*, 8 percent of US companies now offer the benefit of letting employees bring their dogs to work.

There are many benefits to a dog-friendly office. Dogs can help employees feel less stress—something everyone can benefit from. This same study found that employees who brought their dogs to work reported lower levels of stress throughout the day than employees who did not.

Besides that, bringing dogs to work can help increase socialization, connecting people across the company who may not have worked together directly or even met. This can help foster a feeling of community and a more horizontal organizational structure. Dogs can serve as an icebreaker and conversation starter, enabling employees to build more meaningful relationships across the company.

Watching someone notice a dog from across the room and smile, or seeing them laugh as Bennett falls asleep with his tongue out during a long meeting always makes my day. I also love to see Bennett develop personal friendships with my colleagues, and it makes me happy to see how excited he gets to walk into the office each morning.

Dogs help work feel more like home and colleagues feel more like family. What could be more hyggelig than that?

your head, relieve tension, and enable you to feel more hyggelig and refreshed.

Temperature

When we think of places that embody hygge, American offices likely don't make the top of the list for many of us. They are just not known for being cozy. Standard office temperatures, 68 to 76 degrees* Fahrenheit, were set in the 1960s to make men in heavy suits more comfortable. Decades later, dress codes have changed and many American workers are unnecessarily cold and uncomfortable at work.

Still, temperature preferences vary significantly from person to person. Seventy degrees may cause one employee to shiver and another to sweat. Finding a perfect balance that works for everyone can be tricky, but it's crucial for high employee morale and productivity. A Cornell University study found that office temperature can have a direct

---

*This may sound higher than you'd expect, but when you're sitting for hours without moving, these temperatures don't feel the same to your body as when you're taking a walk outside on a spring day of the same temperature.

impact on performance, so it's necessary to find a happy medium.

If you work in an ice-cold environment and have trouble feeling comfortable, let alone hyggeligt, at work, you can take some steps to improve this. If cold air is blasting all day long from the nearest air conditioner vent, politely connect with the office manager to discuss shutting off the vent nearest to your desk or adjusting the temperature, if possible. If your organization allows space heaters, adding one under your desk can make your personal space feel much cozier. If your company policy forbids space heaters (they are known fire hazards),

consider keeping an electric blanket on your desk chair. This will use far less electricity, but it will still make a significant impact. You can also make your office space feel more hyggelig by bringing in a thick blanket, an oversized, cozy scarf, or a warm cardigan or pull-on sweater.

Finally, if your office is cold while the weather is hot, be sure to take breaks throughout the day to step outside, feel the sun, and warm your face and limbs. This can make the AC feel refreshing again and give you a much-needed dose of warm, fresh air.

Social Events

TV shows such as *The Office* and *Parks and Recreation* have tapped into the feel of office politics and employee interactions. The common thread in these shows and other forms of media that feature office life is that office relationships, whether friendly or not, can have a significant impact on your life and happiness. After all, many of us spend 40 or more hours a week with our colleagues—far more time than we're able to spend with friends

and family who we don't live with. So the more hyggelig our office relationships, the better off we are.

Building a positive, fun, social community at work
can help make work feel less like, well, work. While
developing meaningful friendships in the office can
take time, there are many ways to make your experiences with colleagues more hyggelige right away.

Take Advantage of Presented Opportunities.
Does your company offer social benefits, such as
the occasional company outing, happy hour, or
intramural sport teams? Show up for these opportunities when you have the chance. They may seem
cheesy at first, but you'll more than likely make new
friends and connections within the company that
you wouldn't have otherwise. Often, companies
need volunteers to help organize and plan these
events, too, so consider getting involved. You may
even end up feeling a sense of accomplishment and
ownership when the event or activity takes place.

Plan Your Own. You can also infuse hygge into your
work life by creating hyggestunds (hygge-infused
events) with colleagues. For example, you can start
a birthday tradition with your team. The colleague

whose birthday it is will feel special, and the whole team will benefit from the hyggelig experience of celebration and perhaps, cake. (Just be sure you're not asking colleagues to cough up money all the time to buy their colleagues cake if they're not comfortable doing so. There are ways to celebrate that don't involve spending money.) You could also plan potluck lunches once a month for anyone who is interested. People can sign up to bring their favorite dishes, and then everyone can eat together as a group.

Volunteer Together. Consider organizing a fund-raiser or food or clothing drive in the office to help give back to the community. This experience can go miles toward fostering a more hyggelig environment. If possible, look into planning team-building trips around volunteer programs such as Habitat for Humanity, soup kitchens, or community gardens. Volunteering can bring colleagues together around great causes, and it can be both fun and impactful.

Get Out of the Office. Changing your surroundings can go a long way toward having more hyggelige social experiences at work. Instead of running into colleagues in the break room when getting coffee, consider making a point to go out together for coffee or tea. Add the appointment to your calendar like you would any other meeting, so you can both look forward to it.

General Mind-set

With the rise of social media, many people feel an expectation to develop a personal brand and many Americans work side jobs in addition to their full-time careers. Every weekend, #SundayScaries trends on Twitter as people brace themselves to return to busy workweeks and ever-increasing pressure to innovate and surpass goals. Sometimes it can simply feel overwhelming.

My Danish host parents visited me in New York recently, and we chatted about work and careers—over a candlelit dinner, of course. My host father recently became semiretired, an incredible change in his daily life, while my host sister and I are slowly building our own careers and always seem to be looking ahead at the next step. My host mother, Vibeke, who is one of the wisest people I know, said something that stuck with me:

"When you're young, you're constantly looking ahead—to the next day, the weekend, your next vacation, your next promotion, your next job or opportunity. But later in life, you realize how important it is to actually be present in each moment as you live it—not ahead of it."

While you can apply the important concept of staying present in all areas of your life, I find it is especially helpful at work. By taking a hygge mind-set about your career and daily work—staying positive, present, and grateful for each opportunity— you can have a positive attitude from Monday to Friday and beyond.

After I'd had a long, stressful day of work recently, a colleague asked me how I was doing. I admitted I felt overwhelmed and didn't know if I could complete everything on my to-do list. So she asked me, "Can you find the good in this moment? Maybe it's the fact that you have the opportunity to do so much."

When she put it that way, I realized she was right. I was lucky to have the opportunity to balance so many things. I made it through that tough moment by being thankful to have it at all.

So if you're going through a hard day at work— or a hard year—take a hyggelig approach and look for the good. Where is the good in the problem you're having? What are you grateful for? When a day is particularly tough and you have trouble answering that question, you can often say, at the very least, "I learned a lot today." Making even that statement can help you feel better. Did you handle a meeting that went poorly with grace? Did you cheer up a colleague who was having a hard day as well?

Taking on a hygge mind-set and thinking, "I get to do this," instead of, "I have to do this," can truly help.

Lunches and Breaks

We've all rushed to eat lunch at our desks while taking a phone call or finishing a task by a deadline, and—even worse—we've all skipped lunch in the midst of an all-too-busy day. But taking real breaks to eat lunch, take time for yourself, or socialize with colleagues can add hygge to your daily experience at work. Stepping away from your work can help you come back refreshed and ready to take on the next part of your day with a clear head.

Enjoy Your Lunch. As often as possible, try not to eat lunch at your desk while you work. Try to vary where you eat, as well. For example, on one day, you have lunch in a common area with colleagues, and the next day, you can go outside to get a change of scenery and fresh air. If possible, try not to talk or think about work, your next project, or looming deadlines. Instead, focus on your meal or a pleasant conversation. Consider reading a book or article you've been saving, or listen to an inspiring podcast or radio show. By the time you return to your desk, you may be more motivated or have a creative idea you hadn't thought of earlier.

Go Outside. While the weather may not allow this all year long, taking advantage of beautiful weather can have an incredible impact on your mood.

Breathing fresh air and soaking in vitamin D can help you return to your desk feeling all the more rejuvenated and ready to take on your next meeting or project.

Mobile Meetings. Do you have any meetings you could hold while on a walk or coffee run, or over lunch? By mixing up the scenery of your meetings, especially with your direct reports or close colleagues, you can invoke a more hyggelig experience. Take turns buying each other a cup of coffee or find a path to walk that allows you to catch up on projects or goals, brainstorm new ideas, or just connect in a deeper way than you usually do. When you bring hygge into your relationship with your colleagues, even traditional meetings can feel more fun, relaxed, and productive.

Schedule Time. If you have trouble stepping away for a break, schedule time on your calendar to grab a cup of coffee with a colleague or take a walk together. Not only will you have something to look forward to during the rest of your busy day, but you'll also have someone holding you accountable to actually pause and take a break.

Commute

Many of us hate commuting, yet we do it twice a day and at least five days a week. Whether you sit in seemingly endless traffic on your drive to work or take a crowded train with dozens of other travelers, commuting is often an annoying experience, and, unfortunately, this can have a big impact on your mood for the rest of the day. By taking simple steps to make your commute as pleasant and hyggelig as possible, you can kick off each day on a better note.

In Copenhagen, for example, more than 50 percent of the population commutes by bicycle. Instead of facing unpredictable variables like delays, traffic jams, or overcrowded trains, they have complete control over their commute—and they get the added bonuses of fresh air and exercise. In fact, Danes even bike in the rain and snow—they just dress in layers or add waterproof ponchos.

I loved commuting by bike, so when I moved to New York City, maintaining this same quality of commute was important to me. I chose to live in a miniscule apartment in Hell's Kitchen so I could walk to work, I joined a short-term bicycle rental program, and I have taken my commute into

consideration every time I've interviewed for a new job. I can't recommend getting to work this way highly enough if you have the opportunity to live within a reasonable distance of your office. The fresh air and exercise can help you start and end each workday on a high note.

If you don't live close enough to your job do this, there are other ways you can make your commute more hyggelig. Consider carpooling or traveling to work with a friend or neighbor who travels a similar route. Having someone to commute with can give you a fun, social start and end to the day. If possible, try adjusting your start and end times to make for a better commute experience. Often, leaving earlier or later so you can travel on "off-peak" times can help you avoid the crowds and make your trip more pleasant.

If you work from home, take time to get outside at the beginning and end of your day to help transition from home mode to work mode. Whether you go for a walk or run or get a cup of coffee at a local café, this time can help you bookend your workday with hygge.

No matter how you commute, finding a routine that makes you feel great is key to maximizing workday hygge. For example, every morning on my walk to work, I call my mom. We catch up on recent events in our lives, share what our day ahead looks like, and motivate one another to stay positive and focused. It's the best way for me to kick off each morning, and I walk into the office feeling comfort and joy.

If chatting doesn't put you in the right headspace on your commute, then find music or podcasts that can similarly motivate you or make you smile. Daily podcasts are great to help you set a routine and have something to look forward to, or you can look for TV shows that awaken your mind and inspire you to start your day on the right foot. If you ride a train or bus to work, then consider finding books that will put you in a good mood while you travel.

Work-Life Balance

Above all else, balance is the key to hygge in the workplace and in your career. These days, that is much easier said than done. Many of us no longer relate to the concept of a 9-to-5 job. More of us relate to something along the lines of "8 to 7, then I'll log in again later just to finish up a few things." With technology allowing most of us to work from anywhere and stay in contact at any time, global business mind-sets that make it seem like work never sleeps, and the increasing pressure to do something for your career outside of your day job, it can be hard to actually stop working.

However, it's important to pause and truly take time away from work. Focusing on ourselves, our families, our friends, and our passions outside of the office reminds us why we work as hard as we do—to care for the people around us and lead the lives we want.

Here are a few tips for finding a better work-life balance.

Set Boundaries. What can you do to ensure that, the majority of the time, you only work from 9 a.m. to 5 p.m. (or whatever your exact scheduled hours may be)? Basing your to-do list on top priorities, logging out of your email when working on a focus-oriented task, and finding ways to eliminate unnecessary meetings can go a long way in helping you get things done. Then, when you log off for the day, truly log off. Don't continue checking emails or log in at home out of habit. If you need to be accessible in case of something urgent, share with your team and boss how they can reach you if the need arises. This way, instead of regularly checking in and feeling like you're always on, you can get a single text or chat notification when something happens that needs your immediate attention. This can help eliminate the anxious "have I missed anything?" feeling that many of us have grown accustomed to.

Stay Present. When you're not working, make sure your mind stops working, too. Often, I'll find myself reliving a problem at work, stressing about an upcoming deadline, or worrying about work in general for no reason at all—all while sitting at brunch with friends, watching a movie, or relaxing in some other way where work should not be on my radar. If, while you're relaxing, you think of something work related that you want to check up on later, write it down and make a note to look into it first thing when you get back to work the next day. This will help you take it off your mind for now and return to your present moment outside of the office.

Be Prepared to Leave. Ultimately, perhaps your job is just not the right fit for you. We've all been there—and it's not a good feeling. This chapter has outlined a number of ways you can make your work life better, but if you're in a work situation that makes you unhappy every day, no matter how much you've done to feel differently, then you may need to make a bigger change. To prepare for such an occasion, make sure you're saving money in an emergency fund (typically, this should be the equivalent of 6 to 12 months' worth of your cost-of-living expenses). Having the financial freedom to leave a bad work situation means that you are at your current job because you want to be—not because you need to be in order to survive. A hard job or a bad boss can still be a good thing—especially if the position you have is furthering your experience and leading you toward the place you need to be. But if it's terrible and you dread going into work, it's okay to make a change. After all, you only have one life. You deserve to live it well.

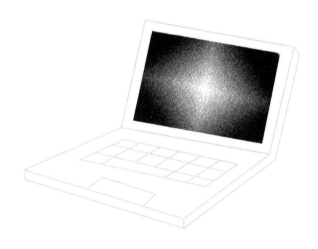

Hygge in the Workplace

Work is an undeniably important part of our lives. It's where we spend much of our time, and where we go to learn, grow, and provide for ourselves and our families. Taking the time to make our work experience more hyggelig can have a positive impact on our overall happiness, as well as our productivity and creativity. It can give us a greater sense of purpose and motivation—all things we can use a little more of on Monday mornings.

Go Forth and Hygge!

Our world is moving at a breakneck pace. A new line of iPhones arrives every fall, advances in technology continue to affect our job market, and our social lives are interrupted by our unconscious "always on" approach to devices and work. The only thing certain about the future is change.

That said, all of the simple things that fill us with peace, warmth, and joy remain constant. A barefoot walk along the beach. Sitting by a crackling fire with a good book. Setting the table for dinner with our family and loved ones. These experiences that warm us from the inside out, that we can't help but smile about whenever we think of them—these moments are true hygge and will stay with us long after we upgrade our iPhones or change jobs.

With this book, my goal was to help you discover a number of ways to build a more hygge life for yourself. From finding a hygge sense of self to incorporating hygge into your home, your community, and your career, I hope you've seen how small

changes and actions can help you feel more hyggelig, and therefore full of joy, every single day.

As you set out to build your most hygge life,
I hope to leave you with one final reminder that
bears repeating. Hygge is, at its core, finding and
appreciating the little things. When you begin to
notice the sweet small details of life, and feel gratitude for them right then and there, you'll know
you're well on your way. It's a little like being nostal-
gic in the moment, rather than after the fact.

Good luck out there, my friends! And please,
don't forget to stop and smell the roses.

Resources

CHAPTER 1

Bilde, Marie. "Of Hype and Hygge: Those Books Aren't Danish." *Publishing Perspectives*, March 9, 2017.

Brooks, Arthur C. "A Formula for Happiness." *New York Times*, December 14, 2013.

Carson, James. "How Much Time are You Spending on Your Smartphone?" Time to Log Off, March 14, 2018. https://www.nytimes.com/2013/12/15/opinion/sunday /a-formula-for-happiness.html

Ducharme, Jamie. "This Is the Amount of Money You Need to Be Happy, According to Research." *Time*, February 14, 2018.

Foster, Ann. "19 Hygge Books Perfect to Curl Up With on a Winter Night." Book Riot, November 27, 2017.

Gilbert, Elizabeth. *Big Magic: Creative Living Beyond Fear.* New York: Riverhead Books, 2016. "How Much Time Do People Spend on Their Phones in 2017?" Hackernoon. https://hackernoon.com/how-much-time-do-people-spend-on-their-mobile-phones-in-2017-e5f90a0b10a6

"IKEA Live Lagom: The Swedish secret to leading a more sustainable life." IKEA.

"ioS 12 Introduces New Features to Reduce Interruptions and Manage Screen Time." Apple News Room, June 4, 2018.

Jensen, K. Thor. "11 Reasons to Stop Looking at Your Phone." *PC Magazine*, April 11, 2017.

Lipsman, Andrew. "Mobile Matures as the Cross-Platform Era Emerges." Comscore blog, March 31, 2017.

Luscombe, Belinda. "Do We Need $75,000 a Year to Be Happy?" *Time*, September 6, 2010.

Marvin, Rob. "Americans Spend Over 11 Hours Per Day Consuming Media." *PC Magazine*, July 31, 2018.

Mineo, Liz. "Good Genes are Nice, But Joy is Better." *The Harvard Gazette*, April 11, 2017.

Molla, Rani, and Kurt Wagner. "People Spend Almost as Much Time on Instagram as They Do on Facebook." Recode, June 25, 2018.

Sukhoterina, Yelena. "iPhone Warns Their Users of Its Biggest Health Risk in Its Manual (What You Need to Know)." AltHealth-WORKS, September 22, 2017.

Walton, Alice G. "6 Ways Social Media Affects Our Mental Health." *Forbes*, June 30, 2017.

"Word of the Year 2016 - Shortlist." The Oxford English Dictionary.

CHAPTER 2

"A Nation of Cyclists." https://denmark.dk/.

"Americans Say They are More Anxious than a Year Ago; Baby Boomers Report Greatest Increase in Anxiety." American Psychiatric Association, May 7, 2018.

Clark, Jodi. "Hygge for Your Health: Benefits of This Cozy Wellness Trend." Very Well Mind, May 8, 2018.

Ducharme, Jamie. "A Lot of Americans Are More Anxious Than They Were Last Year, a New Poll Says." *Time*, May 8, 2018.

"Headspace." Headspace App. https://www.headspace.com /headspace-meditation-app.

"How Many People Meditate?" Mindworks. https://mindworks .org/blog/how-many-people-meditate/.

"How to Hygge Yourself Happy." Yoga for Modern Life, November 1, 2017.

Macmillan, Amanda. "Yoga Is Officially Sweeping the Workplace." *Time*, January 5, 2017.

"Meditation 101: Techniques, Benefits, and a Beginner's How-To." Gaiam. https://www.gaiam.com/blogs/discover /meditation-101-techniques-benefits-and-a-beginner-s-how-to

"Mindfulness Is More Than A Buzzword: A Look Behind The Movement." *Forbes*, September 29, 2017.

"Most Used Mind & Body Practices." Use of Complementary Health Approaches in the U.S., National Health Interview Survey, September 24, 2018. https://nccih.nih.gov/research/statistics /NHIS/2012/mind-body/meditation

"Oprah & Deepak 21-Day Meditation Experience." Chopra Center Meditation. https://chopracentermeditation.com/.

Seppälä, Emma M. "20 Scientific Reasons to Start Meditating Today." *Psychology Today*, September 11, 2013.

"Understand the Facts." Anxiety and Depression Association of America. https://adaa.org/understanding-anxiety.

"Use of Complementary Health Approaches in the U.S.: Most Used Mind & Body Practices: Meditation." National Health Interview Survey, National Center for Complementary and Integrative Health. https://nccih.nih.gov/research/statistics /NHIS/2012/mind-body/meditation.

CHAPTER 3

"Cocoa by Candlelight." *The Economist*, September 29, 2016.

Gekas, Alexandra. "10 Health Benefits of Owning a Pet." *Woman's Day*, February 28, 2011.

Harvard Health Publishing. "Having a Dog Can Help Your Heart - Literally." Harvard Health Blog. Accessed November 15, 2018. https://www.health.harvard.edu/staying-healthy /having-a-dog-can-help-your-heart--literally.

Hook, Cheryl. "The Science of Relaxation: Why Are Candles So Calming?" Melt, December 30, 2016.

"How to Use Color for Good Feng Shui." The Spruce, April 19, 2018.

"How to Use Mirrors to Create Good Feng Shui." The Spruce, August 6, 2018.

Kennedy, Merrit. "How Do Successful People's Sleep Patterns Compare to the Average American?" NPR, December 24, 2015.

Kondō, Marie. The Life-Changing Magic of Tidying Up. Berkeley, California: Ten Speed Press, 2014.

Leasca, Stacey. "One Easy Way to Get a Better Night's Sleep." Travel and Leisure, November 27, 2017.

Magnusson, Margareta. The Art of Swedish Death Cleaning: How to Free Yourself and Your Family from a Lifetime of Clutter. New York: Scribner, 2018.

Prostak, Sergio. "Study: Opening Windows and Doors Improves Sleep Quality." Sci News, November 23, 2017.

Saiidi, Uptin. "Millennials are Prioritizing 'Experiences' Over Stuff." CNBC, last modified May 6, 2016.

Saloman, Laurie. "Can a Pet Help You Defeat Depression." Quality Health, April 6, 2009.

Tchi, Rodika. "How to Create Good Feng Shui in Your Home." The Spruce, last modified November 15, 2018.

Tchi, Rodika. "How to Use Color for Good Feng Shui."
The Spruce, last modified November 17, 2018.

Weber, Kathryn. "The 6 Critical Differences Between Classical Feng Shui and Western Black Feng Shui: Confessions of a Former Black Hat Practitioner." Red Lotus Letter, February 21, 2017.

CHAPTER 4

Cohut, Maria. "What Are the Health Benefits of Being Social?" *Medical News Today*, February 23, 2018.

Fratiglioni, Laura, Stephanie Paillard-Borg, and Bengt Winblad. "An Active and Socially Integrated Lifestyle in Late Life Might Protect against Dementia." The Lancet Neurology 3, no. 6 (June 2004): 343[en dash]353. doi:10.1016/S1474-4422(04)00767-7

"How to Be Better at Parties." *The New York Times*. Accessed November 15, 2018. https://www.nytimes.com/guides/smarterliving/be-better-at-parties.

Tamir, Diana I., and Jason P. Mitchell. "Disclosing Information about the Self Is Intrinsically Rewarding." PNAS. May 22, 2012. Accessed November 15, 2018. http://www.pnas.org/content/109/21/8038.

Troyer, Angela K. "The Health Benefits of Socializing." *Psychology Today*, June 30, 2016.

CHAPTER 5

Foreman, Anne M., Margaret K. Glenn, B. Jean Meade, and Olive Wirth. "Dogs in the Workplace: A Review of the Benefits and Potential Challenges." *International Journal of Environmental Research and Public Health* 14, no. 5 (May 2017): 498. doi:10.3390/ijerph14050498.

Lang, Susan S. "Study links warm offices to fewer typing errors and higher productivity." *Cornell Chronicle*, October 19, 2004.

Index

A

Air, 66, 75
Anxiety, 23–24, 32

B

Balance, 132–135
Baths, 26–29
Bedding, 74
Bedrooms, 73–75
Beverages, 114
Blankets, 63–64
Book clubs, 36
Boundary-setting, 133
Breaks, taking, 126–128
Breathing, 115, 118

C

Candles, 57–58
Children, 98–101
Christmas, 95–96
Clothing, 36–39
Color, 67
Community
    building, 82–83
    fitness and exercise, 47
    and happiness, 12
        workplace, 120–123
Commuting, 129–132
Conversation, 101–103
Cooking, 40–41
Còsagach, 11
Coziness, 2
Creativity, 29–32

D

Décor, 61–64

E

Eating, 39–45, 84–86
Exercise, 45–48

F

Family
    chosen, 91–92
    and happiness, 12
    quality time with, 87–89
Feng shui, 65–67
Fika, 10
Fireplaces, 64
Fjaka, 10

Food and dining, 39–45
Friends, 87–89. *See also*
    Community
Furniture, 62

G
Gezellig, 10
Gilbert, Elizabeth, 29–30

H
Happiness, 12–17
Holidays, 94–98
Home, energy of, 52–56, 79
Hosting, 90, 93–94
Hygge
    and American
        culture, 4–7
    key terms, 7–9
    meaning of, 2–4
    mind-set, 17–18, 137–138

K
Kierkegaard, Søren, 15
Knits, 72

L
Lagom, 10
Letter writing, 103–106

Lighting, 56–60, 66, 75
Lunch, making time
    for, 126–128

M
Mail, 103–106
Massages, 29
Materials, 71–73
Meals, sharing, 41, 84–86
Meditation, 32–34, 58
Mindfulness, 32–34
Minimalism, 68–71
Mirrors, 66–67
Mugs, 114
Music, 114–115

N
Natural light, 60, 66
Natural materials and
    textures, 72

O
Offices, 111–113. *See also*
    Workplaces

P
Personal style, 36–39
Pets, 76–78, 116–117

Philoxenía, 11

Pillows, 62–63

R

Reading, 34–36

Relationships, 82–83, 107, 120–123. *See also* Community; Family; Friends

Rewards, 15

Rugs, 72

S

Saunas, 26–29

Seasons

and clothing, 38–39

and cooking, 41

and space refreshing, 70

Self-care, 23–26, 49

Sheepskin, 73

Shoes, 37–38

Social interactions, 82–84, 107, 120–123. *See also* Conversation

Stress, 23–24

Sweets and treats, 42–43

T

Temperature, 118–120

Textures, 71–73

Thanksgiving, 97–98

Traditions, 94–98

W

Work

and happiness, 13–15, 110–111, 136

-life balance, 132–135

mind-set about, 123–126

Workplaces

atmosphere of, 113–115, 118

desks and cubicles, 111–113

lunches and breaks, 126–128

temperature of, 118–120

Acknowledgments

My gratitude is endless.

To my incredible editors Pippa, Vanessa, Lauren, and the entire Althea Press and Callisto Media teams. Thank you for bringing this book to life.

To my loving parents, Karen and Emile, for their unwavering support. To my brother and best friend, Francesco.

To my amazing host parents, Vibeke and Jens, and my wonderful sister, Mette.

To my Danes: Sara, Signe, Ea, Sofie, Mia, Sidsel, Tanja, Heidi, Kristian, Ole, and Kirsten.

To my Americans: Abigail, Alex, Alycia, Altin, Amy, Amar, Angelina, Armo, Camille, Charisse, Chelsey, Diane, Deb, Em, Haley, Hope, Jason, Jemme, Jen, JoAnn, Josh, Leslie, Mary, Massella, Megan, Noah, Royce, Sadie, Sam, and Victoria.

And, to my very best friend, Bennett.

About the Author

Alexandra Amarotico is a social media and marketing consultant based in New York. She has worked with Fortune 500, fashion, and lifestyle companies, including Warby Parker, Google, Macy's, Coach, Fossil, LearnVest, Lively, and Northwestern Mutual, among others. Alexandra can usually be found biking through the East Village or practicing hygge with her best friend, Bennett, a rambunctious Pomeranian with a heart of gold. You can follow their adventures on Instagram at @sheisred.

CPSIA information can be obtained
at www.ICGtesting.com
Printed in the USA
BVHW092226110119
537646BV00001B/1/P

9 781641 523233